Revealing Difference

Revealing Difference

The Fiction of Isabelle de Charrière

Jenene J. Allison

DELAWARE

Newark: University of Delaware Press
London: Associated University Presses

Associated University Presses
440 Forsgate Drive
Cranbury, NJ 08512

Associated University Presses
25 Sicilian Avenue
London WC1A 2QH, England

Associated University Presses
P.O. Box 338, Port Credit
Mississauga, Ontario
Canada L5G 4L8

The paper used in this publication meets the requirements
of the American National Standard for Permanence of Paper
for Printed Library Materials Z39.48–1984.

Library of Congress Cataloging-in-Publication Data

Allison, Jenene J., 1955–
    Revealing difference : the fiction of Isabelle de Charrière / Jenene J. Allison.
        p. cm.
    Includes bibliographical references and index.
    ISBN 0–87413–566–4 (alk. paper)
    1. Charrière, Isabelle de, 1740–1805--Criticism and interpretation. 2. Women in literature. I. Title.
    PQ1963.C55Z513   1995
    848'.509--dc20   94–48885
                                                                                 CIP

PRINTED IN THE UNITED STATES OF AMERICA

To Shirley

Contents

Acknowledgments

In first place I would like to mention the spirit and enterprise of "les sept," the seven editors of Charrière's *Oeuvres complètes*, whose work has led her so very far from the boundaries of her native Netherlands. With regard to the American context, Alix Deguise deserves recognition for her encouragement of Charrière studies; at a more personal level I am grateful for her kind words while I was struggling to find a voice of my own in the field. Kathy Higgins and Jim Rigdon have been supportive of this project. Many of the chapters in this book started out as conference papers at meetings of various eighteenth-century societies, and I appreciate the comments that I received there. I thank Amelia E. Van Vleck for sharing with me her computer expertise. Insightful comments and criticism offered by Prof. Dorothy Kelly helped to improve the manuscript; I am grateful for the time and thought she gave my work. Finally I thank G. A. van Oorschot for kind permission to use material from the *Oeuvres complètes*.

Introduction

Simone de Beauvoir. Isabelle de Charrière. Andrée Chedid. The alphabetical ordering in a recent "bio-bibliographical source book" on French women writers places Charrière, an eighteenth-century author, in between two outstanding authors of the twentieth century.[1] Now that she is achieving the recognition she deserves, it is satisfying to see her name emerge from lists of neglected women authors for inclusion in a larger category. Dating from a moment of intense significance to the way in which woman is perceived, Charrière's extensive oeuvre proves that she warrants this attention, as she was one most astute readers of women's status in the eighteenth century. The time has come to consider her work in the context of current thought in order to see what such an astute reader can contribute to issues being debated in gender studies today.

Charrière was a Dutch aristocrat of French culture who lived with her husband in Neuchâtel near the border with France. Born in 1740, she lived until 1805, observing from a safe distance the Revolution of 1789, the Terror, and the rise of Napoleon. Although she was not French, like so many well-educated Europeans, she felt French. Writing to her brother Vincent on 28 June 1788, she explained, "C'est leur langue que je parle le mieux c'est leur livres que je connois le mieux c'est avec eux que je suis le plus à mon aise" [It's their language I speak the best, it's their books I know the best, it's with them that I am most comfortable].[2] She is the author of a voluminous correspondence, many political works, a significant number of musical compositions, twenty-six plays, and about eleven short works of fiction. In her novels she tends to address issues of particular relevance to women. One of her letters expresses her sensitivity to women in terms reminiscent of those she used with regard to the French:

Les femmes me sont toujours de quelque chose. Je m'en moque malgré moi plus que des hommes, quand je trouve de quoi me moquer ou plutot quand elles me frapent d'une certaine maniere & je les admire aussi avec plus de transport quand elles me paroissent le meriter. (Letter to Dudley Ryder, 12 January 1789; 3:123)

[Women always interest me. I mock them more than I do men, despite myself, when I find something to mock, or rather when they strike me in a certain way. I also have greater admiration for them when it seems to me they deserve it.]

To appreciate fully the originality of her feminocentric fiction, one must first consider the status of women in late eighteenth-century France.

Both the education of women and their legal status were largely determined by the belief in female biological inferiority and the attribution to woman of responsibility for original sin. However, their negative image was complemented by some positive qualities that were attributed to them. The status of the salons and the popularity of the epistolary novel, forms of social expression for which women were considered to be innately suited, indicate ways in which society valued woman's difference from man. However, all that shines is not gold, and the positive qualities associated with women in the ancien régime actually put them at a disadvantage. Thus, Elizabeth C. Goldsmith points out the traps inherent in valuing the letter-writing skills of women, emphasizing it served to "*reduce* female scriptive authority" since it was based on attributing to them no more than unbridled emotions: in not repressing those emotions, women fell short of moral conduct, and in expressing mere emotion, they fell short of intellectual rigor.[3] Similarly, a *salonnière*, regardless of the degree of influence some of them achieved by running a salon, drew on and never transcended her female identity. For example, while the *salonnière* actually derived increased authority as she became older, unlike other women who were just perceived as less attractive, this larger authority, as Madelyn Gutwirth notes, "might generate male hostility" precisely because it derived from a woman.[4] To prize woman's innate capacity for excelling as letter writer or *salonnière* served to paint woman's confinement to her boudoir or salon as destiny and to perpetuate, albeit in positive terms, the essentialist characterization defining her as inherently different from man. Compelling arguments such as those put forth in Jean-Jacques Rousseau's *Emile, ou de l'Éducation* (Emile, or on education) (1762) added force to this interpretation of the difference between men and women, an interpretation that would be reflected in postrevolutionary legislation.

During the social transformation brought about by the French Revolution, the ideology that attributed to woman an innate predisposition for the roles of either letter writer or *salonnière* was used to justify the actual exclusion of women from the political arena.[5] The essentialist definition of woman became a political issue during the course of the French Revolution. Proponents of women's rights wanted to capitalize on the natural equality of man that was being proclaimed everywhere and wanted to use it for their arguments advancing woman's political equality. But this line of reasoning proved to be ineffective because it could also be manipulated to assert woman's natural inferiority.[6] Following different angles, scholars like Carole Pateman, Dorinda Outram, and Lynn Hunt have chronicled how the social meaning of woman's difference was given a definitive and negative form in the course of the Revolution and its long aftermath.[7]

Today, as the twentieth century draws to a close, we confront in our turn the issue of woman's difference but do so in the context of increasingly complex controversies surrounding women. Some of these controversies are due to developments in medical technologies that were undreamt-of in the eighteenth century. Is it nonetheless possible that an eighteenth-century author's assessment of woman's difference could help to clarify what is at stake in the arguments being so urgently proclaimed at this moment? Certainly the history of the French Revolution seems to have become one chapter in the history of gender. Historian Karen Offen proposes that "an understanding of the processes of sexual politics in the French Revolution ... enables us not only to appreciate the complete shape of our past but also enhances the possibilities for shaping our future differently."[8] Perhaps, then, the issue is not whether it is possible but rather how the eighteenth century can serve the twentieth. *Revealing Difference* has been written to show that Charrière is ideally suited to serve as just such a bridge between the errors of the past and the chances for the future.

In seeking a way to theorize gender that neither traps women and men in roles based on anatomy nor conflates them into one unsexed category of postmodern subjects, critics face the problematic alternative of essentialism versus poststructuralism.[9] In our thinking about woman, should we privilege her difference from man or their ressemblance to one another? A diversity of approaches to this question may be found within Charrière's fiction. Her novels, frequently interpreted as contesting woman's perilous lack of autonomy, articulate what amount to radical claims on behalf of women but in seemingly anodine forms, illustrating how the novel, in the hands of a perspicacious author, might serve as a more effective vehicle for social change than might any type of explicit criticism.

Revealing Difference is meant to be read in two different ways. First of all, it points to Charrière's own revealing difference from other authors. Her fiction diverges from the dominant trends in French literature of the eighteenth century. In addressing what is particular about Charrière, I draw on the methods of a feminist criticism designed to elucidate the ways in which not just plot but narrative form may serve to perpetuate patriarchal structures. To the extent that one can subscribe to a point of view that posits itself as a refutation of a single point of view, I subscribe to Annette Kolodny's notion of a pluralistic literary criticism. She argues for "an acute and impassioned *attentiveness* to the ways in which primarily male structures of power are inscribed (or encoded) within our literary inheritances."[10] I am concerned, then, not only with Charrière's creation of unconventional heroines, for example, but also with the treatment of genre evident in her oeuvre. The second meaning of *Revealing Difference* points to the way in which Charrière's novels uncover with acuity the consequences of how woman's difference from man is interpreted. These texts raise issues that remain unresolved today and that distinguish different ways of theorizing gender.

In the pages that follow, I begin with Charrière's treatment of heroines and then progress to a consideration of larger theoretical issues.[11] Chapter 1 presents her variations on the theme of the heroine whose father opposes her choice of spouse.[12] These are the heroines of "Le Noble" [The nobleman], *Lettres trouvées dans des porte-feuilles d'émigrés* [Letters found in the satchels of émigrés], and *Sainte Anne*. In striking contrast to the eighteenth-century heroine as she is presented in surveys of the feminocentric novel, those of Charrière tend to overcome paternal prohibition.[13] But this author is not distinctive simply because her heroines attain what they seek. What is important in the three texts studied here is that the literary means depicting their success undermine in different ways repressive images of women. The effect is to counter stereotypes prevalent in feminocentric novels and in society more generally. For one heroine, success will be out of the question, and chapter 2 concerns the special case of a doomed heroine. The negative representation of the heroine in *Henriette et Richard* [Henriette and Richard] results from the nature of the oppositional father she confronts. The way in which he becomes empowered at her expense could be used to illustrate Pateman's reading of the social contract instituted by the Revolution as "a sexual contract which constitutes men's patriarchal right over women." [14] As a literary figure, the bourgeois individual who is Henriette's father represents so absolute an obstacle to her aspirations that he makes aristocratic oppositional fathers appear relatively tractable. Although this novel seems unfinished, it is all too conclusive, given the nature of the impasse confronted by the heroine.

The innovative aspect of Charrière's work exceeds her treatment of the heroine, and chapter 3 addresses the larger issue of discourse from a focus pertinent to gender theory. Identifying the way in which a given discourse, be it scientific or literary, is gendered exposes yet one more manifestation of the feminine/masculine opposition. In the historical and philosophical evolution of this opposition — what Hélène Cixous calls "a universal battlefield" — the feminine has always been devalued as secondary. [15] Chapter 3 covers two novels: *Lettres écrites de Lausanne* [Letters written from Lausanne] and *Sir Walter Finch et son fils* [Sir Walter Finch and his son]. These novels expose the gendered nature of two types of discourse: the monophonic epistolary novel, a genre marked as feminine, and the philosophe's language, a form marked as masculine. The masculine/feminine opposition draws on the reality of the physical difference between women and men, and to illustrate how this difference is treated in Charrière's fiction, I focus next on three novels in which pregnancy is a factor. In chapter 4, then, I read *Lettres de Mistriss Henley* [Letters of Mistress Henley], *Lettres neuchâteloises* [Letters from Neuchâtel], and *Trois femmes* [Three women], with particular attention to Luce Irigaray's assessment of the meaning assigned by Western culture to woman's capacity for pregnancy. The images of woman that emerge from these novels engage at a crucial point the ongoing debate over theorizing a universal, transcendental Woman versus minimizing this category. This same debate informs the exploration of feminist biography. Should the biography of a woman be organized around the significance to all women of her experience as a woman? If so, an essentialist definition of woman is implied, one susceptible to the criticism of promoting the unified self that has been the target of so much contemporary criticism. From an alternative point of view, the essentialist definition of woman may also be condemned for insensitivity to differences of race, class, and sexual orientation. Should the biography of a woman perhaps be organized around a deconstructionist approach? If so, how could it possibly be empowering for women? In my last chapter, I use both a segment from her correspondence and her early self-portrait, "Zélide," to propose two perspectives on how Charrière's biography may be conceptualized. By way of conclusion, I read Charrière's unfinished and fragmentary *Asychis ou le Prince d'Egypte* [Asychis, or the prince of Egypt] as a literary model for speaking about women.

The translations, except for *Lettres de Mistriss Henley*, are my own. I have not modernized the spelling or the punctuation of quotations drawn from Charrière's *Oeuvres complètes*.

Revealing Difference

1

New Heroines:
Countering Women's Fiction(s)

The success of *Lettres portugaises* [The letters of a Portuguese nun] (1669), probably authored by Gabriel de Guilleragues (d. 1685), illustrates well the way in which representations of women can serve to perpetuate a stereotype of woman.[1] This brief, monophonic epistolary novel presents the letters of an abandoned Portuguese nun to the French officer who seduced her. So great was the appeal of the novel *Lettres portugaises* that the term "une portugaise" came to designate the standard abandoned-woman's passionate letter. That the title should be so readily adapted for current usage in seventeenth-century France reflects a receptivity to the image of woman implied by such a form.[2] The novel itself, in part because of the question of authorship, has been the focus of debates concerning the idea of a female voice.[3] The woman pouring her emotions into a letter was a woman in thrall to her passion, and this image reflected the notion that women, being closer to nature, were less able than men to repress passion. The literary form that received the name "une portugaise," and the image of woman that informed it, are intimately linked; indeed they are "entangled," to use Nancy K. Miller's metaphor. Speaking of our need to rewrite the history of the novel, she proposes "look[ing] ... at the sites where the intersecting discourses on femininity (as the inflected term of the masculine-feminine couple) and fiction become — like the recklessly heterosexual couples of the social text they also articulate — permanently and dangerously entangled."[4] The complexity of this relationship between femininity and fiction structures the heroine in the eighteenth-century novel.[5] Relative to these conventional figures, Charrière's heroines seem at first glance quite

19

innovative. Considered more closely, they are better described as refutations of the conventional.

Miller's *The Heroine's Text: Readings in the French and English Novel, 1722–1782* has become a point of reference for eighteenth-century fiction, although she has moved beyond the critical approach employed in this survey.[6] She sorts the eight canonical novels she examines into two categories: "euphoric" plots, in which the female protagonist rises gloriously to "integration into society" through marriage, and "dysphoric" plots, in which she falls tragically into the abyss of death or exile. "The heroine's text is plotted within this ideologically delimited space of an either/or closure, within the conventional rhetoric of the sociolect."[7] The literary convention of such plots parallels the social forces confining women to one type of role — that of spouse, a role that was itself confining. Reflecting on this, Margaret Higonnet wonders if the distinction between the two types of plots is not perhaps paradoxical since "a marriage without describable future" may well be "more static and fatal to its heroine" than the more obviously tragic conclusion in a dysphoric plot.[8] In the three texts I discuss here, Charrière plots her protagonists along the euphoric line leading to marriage. However, by the conclusion of each novel, the conventional plot has been modified because it has been articulated so that a stereotypical image of woman is first presented and then undermined.

Not only does the euphoric plot undergo a subtle alteration, the heroines themselves are described with atypical attributes.[9] Pierre Fauchery's monumental *La Destinée féminine dans le roman européen du dix-huitième siècle: 1713–1807* catalogues female protagonists, and among all the variants and possibilities that he lists, there are certain attributes that appear consistently. The common denominator, according to Fauchery, is that woman "remains an eternal minor," the fictional heroines reflecting the "original vice of *being a woman.*"[10] While he does include Charrière in his monumental survey, the sheer number of characters considered causes him to assimilate her characters into a model that is oversimplified.[11] To free these characters from such a reductive classification, I compare three versions of the same type (the heroine progressing according to a euphoric plot). The heroines in "Le Noble" (1763), *Lettres trouvées dans des porte-feuilles d'émigrés* (1793), and *Sainte Anne* (1799) are all of this type yet significantly different from this type. These three novels also feature the device of a letter that is either not written or not read. This device is of particular interest because of the cultural implications of the association between women and letter writing in the eighteenth century. Letter writing was not authoritative; as Elizabeth J. MacArthur notes, "Women could write letters without considering themselves, and without being considered by others, as authors."[12] In addition, letter writing was confined, like women, to the private sphere. In this chapter I will pursue the various facets of the link between women and letter writing as it is represented in Charrière's fiction.[13] Through a close reading of a letter-writing scene in each novel, we will see that the representation of an apparently conventional heroine may serve to weaken the force of literary convention itself.

Countering the Wrong Image

The first work by the then unmarried Isabelle van Tuyll is "Le Noble" (8:19–34). Like Voltaire's "Candide" (1759) it is often ironical and consistently sharp in its criticism of the old nobility. The problem presented in "Le Noble" is a classic one: Julie loves Valaincourt, but her father, the Baron d'Arnonville, prohibits the marriage because the young man's family has been noble for only one generation. The characters are clearly delineated in terms of good and bad: those who oppose the young lovers are incarnations of blind prejudice; the lovers are complex, appealing individuals. The Baron d'Arnonville, for example, is an idiot, "ne pensant pas que la parfaite inutilité fût indigne de la haute naissance, ni que ce fût déroger que n'être bon à rien" (22) [not believing that absolute uselessness was unworthy of high birth, nor that it was ignoble to be good for nothing].[14] Both Julie and Valaincourt have the necessary attributes of physical beauty, but in addition to this quality, their relationship is described with the sort of titillating innuendo that was so frequently condemned in the novel of the eighteenth century. While visiting Valaincourt's family, Julie bumps into him one evening in the dark hallway and they kiss for the first time: "Alors Valaincourt prit un baiser à Julie, & Julie qui n'aimoit pas à refuser ce qu'elle pouvoit donner sans peine, le laissa prendre" (23) [Then Valaincourt took a kiss from Julie, and Julie, who didn't like to refuse what she could easily give away, let it be taken]. The way in which the characters are drawn, and the fact that it is the joys of young love that are threatened by aristocratic prejudice, all seem to make of "Le Noble" an indictment of the aristocracy.

On the other hand, a more attentive reading of "Le Noble" makes classifying it as pure antiaristocratic propaganda problematic. The quotation Charrière placed on the title page is: "On ne suit pas toujours ses aïeux ni son père" [One does not always follow one's ancestors or one's father] from "L'Education" by La Fontaine (one of her favorite authors). [15] The fable is important, for the moral is that unless one cultivates both one's talents and skills, a well-born person can easily degenerate into a despicable being. In "Le Noble," then, Charrière, would not so much be condemning the aristocracy in the figure of the Baron d'Arnonville as using him to suggest that the aristocracy needs renewal and fresh blood. This is confirmed by the description of how Valaincourt's father, through his conduct and his good deeds, became noble: "Les Sages diroient que quand c'est de cette façon qu'on a acquis la noblesse, la plus nouvelle est la meilleure, que le premier noble de sa race doit être le plus glorieux d'un titre dont il est l'auteur" (23) [Wise men would say that when it is in this manner that one has acquired nobility, the most recent is the best, that the first nobleman of his line ought to be the most proud of a title of which he is the author]. Such an interpretation can be further supported by the argument that Charrière makes in *Lettres écrites de Lausanne*, written twenty-three years after "Le Noble." In this novel, the female narrator digresses at one point to elaborate on her idea for what might be termed an aristocratic meritocracy. While maintaining the basic structure of three distinct classes, she would ennoble the children of all the members of the governing council so as to replace noble families on the verge of extinction (8:142). [16]

Given this concern for the perpetuation and even amelioration of aristocratic bloodlines, "Le Noble" might represent a plea that the aristocracy be preserved. After all, Charrière does have Julie return to her father. When he arranges for Julie's brother to marry a loathsome but eminently noble woman, there is a wedding celebration; Julie and Valaincourt sneak in and are forgiven by her father, "lorsque le vin commençoit à confondre dans sa tête l'ancienne, & la nouvelle Noblesse" (34) [when the wine began to muddle up the ancient and the recent nobility in his mind]. In this conclusion, we see that Charrière's explicit condemnation of the aristocracy in "Le Noble" is attenuated by her belief in some aspects of it. However, her rejection of a typical feminine destiny for her protagonist is not similarly attenuated. With her choice of a standard eighteenth-century plot based on a daughter's rebellion against her father's authority, Charrière set up her female protagonist in a situation that could easily lend itself to the euphoric/dysphoric alternative. Although the author does resolve Julie's dilemma with marriage, the conclusion is atypical because it involves a loss of status for her. As Fauchery explains, the eighteenth-century novel tends towards *invraisemblance* by consistently returning one or both young lovers to their original social rank.[17] In the case of "Le Noble," the concluding moral of the story — "Julie fut heureuse et ses Fils ne furent point Chevaliers" (34) [Julie was happy and her sons were not knights] — places the focus on the simultaneity of the woman's happiness and her violation of social conventions.[18]

To appreciate the subversive nature of this text, we need to ask, How does Julie escape the typical feminine destiny? How does Charrière plot her heroine's escape from the physical and social structures oppressing her? In her description of Julie's evolution from "daughter oppressed by her father" to "woman married to the man of her choice," Charrière presents two possible solutions to the dilemma of her protagonist: the first one involves a fake genealogy, the second one an elopement. Julie will accede to the freedom to marry against her father's wishes only after the wrong solution has been rejected. By setting up and rejecting this wrong solution — a solution that, by the terms of the plot alone might have led to the same conclusion — "Le Noble" devalues a stereotype of woman.

The first attempt at solving Julie's dilemma has a catastrophic result: her incarceration. Upon being asked by the Baron the all-important question about Valaincourt's ancestry, Julie had improvised and claimed that he was descended from ancient and impeccable bloodlines (26). Realizing that her father's discovery of her lie would imperil her chances to wed Valaincourt, Julie resolves to write to the young man so that together they could forge a fake genealogy to implant (or transplant) him firmly into the aristocratic order. This letter-writing scene is crucial to the assessment of Charrière's female protagonist because it so clearly represents the stereotypical image of woman that is countered in the conclusion to "Le Noble."

Elle prit l'écritoire, les plumes, & le papier; elle imagina le moyen de faire parvenir sa lettre, & je jurerois qu'elle auroit écrit si elle eût été sure de son stile, & de son ortographe; mais Julie passa légérement sur ses véritables motifs de ne point écrire; elle se persuada en remettant tout cet attirail que la prudence, la réserve, la modestie, le respect des bienséances, l'arrêtoient, & elle s'applaudit des vertus qu'elle n'avoit pas. (27)

[She took the writing desk, the quills, and the paper; she imagined the means by which to have her letter delivered, and I swear she would have written if she had been sure of her style and of her spelling; but Julie glossed over her real motives for not writing. She persuaded herself, while putting away all this equipment, that caution, reserve, modesty, respect for good behavior, were stopping her and she congratulated herself on virtues she didn't have.]

Julie's action here hardly qualifies as an event since it turns into a non-event: after the precise description of her preparations for writing, Julie fails to do so. The value of the scene is as an image rather than as an element advancing the plot. The image presented is of the stereotypical woman, and the details given here describe with accuracy this stereotype. First and foremost, woman is superficial, a creature of appearances. In the eighteenth century, as Landes explains, femininity was taken to be the opposite of reason; it was "pleasure, play, eroticism, artifice, style, politesse, refined facades, and particularity."[19] This is reflected in Julie's primary concern about her letter: its style and spelling as opposed to its content. Secondly, woman is incapable of moral conduct. In the words of one authority on "the woman question," Diderot, one must never forget that because of women's lack of intellectual capacity, they have no profound comprehension of anything, and "les idées de justice, de vertu, de vice, de bonté, de méchanceté nagent à la superficie de leur âme" [the ideas of justice, virtue, vice, good, and evil hover at the furthest reaches of their soul].[20] Thus, even in the privacy of her own thoughts, Julie lies about her motivation for not writing, attributing this motivation to morality (spelled out, rather to excess, in a lengthy list) so that she may proudly congratulate herself on "virtues she didn't have." That it is the narrator who, in juridical terms, authenticates Julie's duplicity ("I swear") further reinforces it; truth can only come from outside the innermost thoughts of the woman presented in this image.[21]

The letter-writing scene acquires a negative quality by the result it generates: Julie's incarceration. The image of Julie at her writing desk, an image that concretizes the stereotype of woman, leads to a betrayal scene duplicating this image. Not knowing that Julie had concocted a magnificent bloodline for him, the love-sick Valaincourt, when confronted by the Baron, blurted out the truth about his ancestry in the course of a hyperbolic protestation of his love for the young noblewoman (28). Valaincourt's description of what he had done wrong is significant. He did not blame himself for being honest but for betraying Julie's *dis*honesty. His error was in failing to assume that a woman would, naturally, lie: "Je devois deviner, je devois me taire.... Ah! c'est pour moi que vous êtes coupable, & c'est moi qui vous trahis!" [I ought to have guessed, I ought to have kept quiet.... Ah! It's for me that you're guilty and it's me who is betraying you!] Upon learning from Valaincourt of Julie's duplicity, the Baron imprisons her in the castle.

A different solution to her dilemma must be found. Unlike the fake genealogy, the solution involving an elopement reverses the type of deceptive speech act that led to Julie's confinement, and it will successfully solve her dilemma. Having persuaded the gardener's daughter to carry messages to his loved one, Valaincourt plans Julie's escape from the castle so that they may elope. However, in contrast to the betrayal scene, where Julie appeared in her role as a stereotype — a superficial, duplicitous creature — here she will be made to appear as a woman of her word, and this is what will precipitate her freedom. An integral component of the plan for her physical escape is Valaincourt's decision to take Julie at her word. He concludes the letter planning their elopement, "Je ne demande point de réponse, vous m'avés dit que vous m'aimiés, c'étoit tout me promettre" (31) [I am not asking for an answer, you told me that you loved me, that was to promise me all]. Julie, for her part, reiterates Valaincourt's confidence that she will be true to her word. The idea that she could be true to her word presents a different image than that in the letter-writing scene, where the narrator drew the reader's attention to Julie's dishonest assessment of her reasons for not writing ("virtues she didn't have"). In "Le Noble," then, a pernicious stereotype of woman is undermined in the course of what appears to be an antiaristocratic satire. An apt metaphor for the text is provided by the basket that concealed Valaincourt's letter. The letter, in which he takes Julie at her word, had been delivered in a basket that eluded the vigilance of Julie's guardian because the guardian assumed it was innocuous; the old woman failed to suspect "la vertu secrete de la corbeille" (30) [the secret virtue of the basket]. This image of a woman as true to her word is "the secret virtue" of the text.

Furthermore, Charrière's protagonist frees herself not just from a physical prison but from the patriarchal structure that legitimated her confinement. To escape from her father's castle, Julie must cross the moat, and she uses portraits of her grandfathers, not of her grandmothers, to do so.[22]

> Le Grand-pere fut jetté dans la boue, & celui-là ... fut suivi d'un second, & puis d'un troisieme. Jamais Julie n'avoit cru qu'on pût tirer si bon parti des Grands-peres.... [L]e visage d'un de ses Ancêtres ... se romp sous ses pieds. (32–33)

> [The grandfather was thrown in the mud and that one ... was followed by a second and then a third. Never had Julie believed one could profit so well from grandfathers.... (T)he face of one of her ancestors ... cracks under her feet.][23]

Jean Starobinski sees in this blasphemous act what he terms a symbolic murder of the father.[24] Another scholar is more critical of Charrière's audacious treatment of grandfathers, pointing to the poor taste and lack of respect in the moat-crossing scene.[25] I read the destruction of these portraits, icons of her confinement, as a way to distance Julie from all that is implied by the image of woman as a solitary letter writer. This heroine, in exceeding the limits of the stereotypical woman, both overcomes her father's opposition to the young man of her choice and symbolically steps outside the patriarchal order to create an identity of her own making.[26]

The wrong solution to Julie's dilemma — one that would have reinforced the patriarchal order by supplying a genealogy for Valaincourt and by determining Julie's identity within this order — has been rejected. We should read her father's condemnation of her accordingly: "Vous mérités bien peu d'être née ce que vous êtes!" (29) [How little you merit having been born what you are!]. In the context of a satire on the aristocracy, we would understand her to have been "born" an aristocrat, but in the context of a feminocentric parable, she was "born" a woman. Through the subversive reimaging of Charrière's protagonist, a way out of the social structure that limits woman to being what she was born is delineated. The key difference between Charrière's text and novels featuring heroines in their role as "eternal minor[s]" is the presence of a challenge to the image of woman that elicited oppressive customs and laws.

In "Le Noble," the plot not only presents a successful heroine but counters a repressive stereotype of woman. The next text under consideration, *Lettres trouvées dans des porte-feuilles d'émigrés*, features a female protagonist who will be as successful as Julie. Here, however, Charrière sets up two heroines in the daughter-versus-father power struggle, and the effect is to undermine the stereotype of woman in a different way: namely, through the suppression of one protagonist in favor of another.

Privileging the Right Heroine

Lettres trouvées is a two-part, polyphonic epistolary novel set in both the London of the French aristocrats who had fled from the threat of the guillotine, the émigrés, and the battlegrounds where the revolutionary and counterrevolutionary armies faced each other. Under the entry for "Charrière" in the *Bloomsbury Guide to Women's Literature,* the work is classified as a text in which Charrière "looks at the causes of the Revolution, and includes a project for a Constitution."[27] In this novel, Charrière permits herself to give vent to her political opinions, and so it is not surprising to find that the fierceness with which she consistently blamed both sides for their equal share in the suffering appears in the novel as an insistence on depicting in detail the pain proper to both. She describes the dismay felt by the lower class in confronting a weak, useless, needlessly cruel aristocracy, as well as the horror of the upper class in facing an irrational, greedy, destructive mob. In addition to the two fighting parties, Charrière focuses on the émigrés in exile, although with less compassion, due no doubt to her well-known impatience with them. Living in Neuchâtel, one of the passageways of the emigration, she was exposed to too many self-pitying, displaced aristocrats to have much sympathy for them.[28] However, an attentive reading of this novel will show that, as with "Le Noble," where the apparent satire of the aristocracy coexists with a more subversive topic, the theme of the war between the various political factions in no way exhausts *Lettres trouvées*. The flux in political hierarchy triggered by the Revolution leads ultimately to posing the question, at the end of the novel, What can the status of woman be now?

The love story in this text is structured like that in "Le Noble," but this one involves two sets of lovers. The Marquis de *** has safely tucked away one daughter, Germaine, in London with some other émigrés so that he may do battle against the revolutionaries. Pauline, another daughter (from a different marriage), remains in their besieged castle in France. Predictably, both young women have formed alliances that are unsuitable because of the political situation. Germaine loves Alphonse, an aristocrat who has refused to join the war on behalf of "la Royauté, la noblesse, & la foi" (8:437) [royalty, nobility, and the faith] as her father defines it. Alphonse is described as so horrified by the inhuman violence of the Revolution that he could not close his eyes to the bloodshed long enough to view it as a political conflict in which one faction might be philosophically superior to the other (439). For her part, Pauline falls in love with L. B. Fonbrune, a republican on the wrong side of "royalty, nobility, and the faith."

The focus of the novel is largely on Germaine's love story; she faces her father's disapproval of her inappropriate choice of spouse whereas Pauline is not shown in this situation. In addition, while Germaine is featured in *Lettres trouvées* both as a character and as an author of letters (in fact, the first letter is hers), Pauline is featured as a character only: she is represented through description and reported dialogue in the letters of Fonbrune and later, in the sequel (*Lettres trouvées dans des porte-feuilles d'émigrés, suite*), in a remarkable letter from a servant in Holland that concludes the novel. Because the sequel has only six letters compared to the twenty-four of the previous section, and because it seems to end *in medias res*, the text might be deemed unfinished. On the contrary, an inherent coherence emerges from a focus on the heroines, making *Lettres trouvées* conclusive as it stands. Over the course of the novel, Germaine recedes into the background after having been the heroine of the first part, and Pauline, previously a background figure, comes to occupy the center of attention. As Germaine is progressively silenced while Pauline acquires more and more a voice of her own, a new image of woman comes to efface an older, more stereotypical one.

Germaine's letters serve primarily to describe the dizzying idleness of the dispossessed émigrés until the occurrence of the event that forces her to address her father's disapproval of Alphonse; at this point, the topic of woman displaces that of revolutionary turmoil. The duchess in charge of Germaine is an arrogant busybody who feels she must not only protect but also control the ward entrusted to her (440). Intercepting a letter from Alphonse, the duchess officiously forwards it to the marquis. Germaine's reaction to this theft is significant because it makes of her the stereotype of woman. Upon discovering what the duchess has done, and in fear of her father's reprisals, Germaine writes a letter to Alphonse, and once again we see the heroine in a letter-writing scene. In fact, this letter-writing scene, occurring as it does within a letter, is even more overdetermined by the association of women with letter writing. Furthermore, as in "Le Noble," no actual letter results from the scene, making the scene's value more visual than narrative. In *Lettres trouvées*, however, the heroine is not seen making the preparations to write but instead is seen imagining a letter — namely, her own version of the real one from Alphonse. Germaine endows this imaginary letter of hers with great power.

> C'était l'heure de faire ma toilette. Victoire m'a habillée comme on habillerait une figure de bois; & sans que je m'apperçusse seulement de ce qu'elle faisait. Je cherchai à me rappeller *tout ce que je vous avais écrit*, & à m'imaginer tout ce que vous aviez pu me répondre, & après *m'être fait* une Lettre de vous, dont je voyais distinctement le pli, les marges, l'écriture, la signature; je voyais mon pere l'ouvrir, se fâcher, lire, rêver & s'appaiser peu-à-peu.... La poupée habillée, on l'a fait descendre & se mettre à table. Il y avait beaucoup de monde. (446–47; emphasis added)

> [It was time for my toilette. Victoire dressed me as one would a stick figure and without my even noticing what she was doing. I tried to remember *everything I had written to you* and to imagine every way that you could have answered me. After having *made myself* a letter from you, a letter whose fold, margins, handwriting, and signature I saw distinctly, I saw my father open it, become angry, read on, daydream, and little by little calm down.... The doll having been dressed, she was made to go downstairs and to be seated at the table. There were a lot of people.]

Germaine specifies that the basis of her letter is "everything I had written to you," and that the resulting letter is one she "made myself." This means that although she is imagining a letter from a man, this letter is not a man's; it is her own creation. Indeed, it must be, since she has never laid eyes on the letter from Alphonse that was sent off on a detour to Germaine's father by the duchess.

It seems that the expression of her father's power over Germaine, manifested through the duchess's capacity to appropriate what belongs rightfully to her ward, brings out Germaine's status as mere object; the labels "stick figure" and "doll" frame the letter-writing scene. The scene with the young woman imagining a letter, like the scene with Julie not writing one, draws on and contributes to a certain image of woman. The passivity with which Germaine confronts the crisis, taking no action except to fantasize, while stereotypically feminine, can in no way serve to free her from the constraint under which she lives. Her passivity is brought out in the telling contrast between the list she uses to describe her imagined letter and the one she uses to describe the effect of this letter. While she emphasizes the concrete or physical attributes of her imagined letter, the "fold, margins, handwriting, and signature," the list of actions she attributes to her father ranges from his opening the letter to his having a change of heart after he daydreams about it. The progression from concrete details to daydreaming, which together add up to Germaine's formula for obtaining what she wants, completes the picture of her reaction as feminine. By the way in which she reacts to a threat to her freedom — with passivity, evident in the decision to imagine rather than to act, and the valorization of daydreaming, as opposed to logical argumentation, for example — she acts out a stereotype of woman prevalent in the eighteenth-century novel.

Clearly such a stick figure/doll could not be expected to liberate herself. Instead of achieving the freedom to marry the man of her choice, Germaine has it given to her without having to smash any graven images of her male ancestors. A way she can both conform to her father's wishes and marry the man she loves is developed when her father undergoes precisely the change of heart about which she had fantasized. In fact, if we follow the letter intercepted by the duchess, we will find that the father's response to this real letter from Alphonse is remarkably close to Germaine's fantasy. What is significant is that he makes a comment about the intercepted letter that serves to mock the conceit underlying the novel itself.

Forgiving his daughter for her clandestine correspondence with a man of whom he disapproved, the marquis graciously admits the letter is from a nice young man. Instead of punishing her, he grants her a voice: "Dans le choix d'un époux comme dans toute autre chose, il faut voir par vos propres yeux, & puis ne prendre un parti qu'avec mon consentement" (452) [In the choice of a spouse, as in all other matters, you must see through your own eyes and then follow a course of action only with my consent]. However, the marquis also refers to what was done by

Germaine's guardian in London: "Je ne sais comment remercier la Duchesse de son zèle; intercepter une Lettre, la détourner de son chemin & lui en faire prendre un si différent, ne m'entrerait jamais dans l'esprit" (451) [I do not know how to thank the duchess for her zeal. To intercept a letter, to divert it from its route and make it take such a different one, would never enter my mind]. And yet, is this not the very conceit upon which is based the eighteenth-century convention of epistolary novels presented as found letters? Of all Charrière's epistolary novels (*Lettres neuchâteloises*, *Lettres écrites de Lausanne*, *Lettres de Mistriss Henley*), none makes so blatant a reference to this conceit: the title *Lettres trouvées dans des porte-feuilles d'émigrés* evokes a scene in which an editor accidentally finds a satchel of letters, probably in his attic or in an old trunk. When the marquis mocks what the duchess did with Alphonse's letter, his comment serves to mock the conceit inherent in the title of Charrière's novel. Through the irony in the marquis's comment, the conformity of *Lettres trouvées* to a literary convention is implied. It is pertinent that the heroine simultaneously acquires the freedom to marry as she wishes. The formulation of the heroine's success in this text differs sharply from that presented in "Le Noble." Where Julie found a way to bypass her father's power, Germaine remains at the disposal of her father. Where "Le Noble" undermined the stereotype of woman, this first part of *Lettres trouvées* confirms it. The most important difference is the addition in the latter of a reference that may direct the reader's attention to what is purely conventional in the text, a category into which the heroine falls. Although a successful heroine, Germaine is not an unconventional one: she is just a woman who does what her father tells her to do.

  In the course of the transition from the first part to the sequel, Germaine recedes into the background as Pauline becomes more important. The first part ends with the discussion of the marquis's efforts to acquire safe passage for his wife and Pauline out of France. *Lettres trouvées dans des porte-feuilles d'émigrés, suite* begins with what will be Germaine's last letter, a letter that is superficial at best. Germaine writes from the countryside to inform Alphonse that she is in "la plus noble, la plus grave, la plus solitaire des retraites" [the most noble, the most solemn, the most solitary of retreats] but that she will not offer him a description because it would be "trop semblable aux descriptions de Romans" (475) [too similar to descriptions found in novels]. She then describes it. Her character seems to fade away in the void of this verbiage, and she will not appear again. The extreme difference between Germaine and Pauline is brought out by the sequel, and the effect of switching from one rather colorless character to a more compelling one is to privilege the latter as heroine. In order to appreciate this contrast, it is necessary to trace the evolution of Pauline.

The best introduction to Pauline is to show what she is not and what she becomes.[29] A German friend was planning a sequel to *Lettres trouvées,* and Charrière foresaw that an author other than herself would pervert the character of Pauline: "Je vois que cela deviendra un roman tragique, Laurent [Fonbrune] poura bien être guillotiné. a la bonne heure. Pauline peut-être se noyera, soit" (412) [I see that it will become a tragic novel. Laurent (Fonbrune) might well be guillotined; why not. Perhaps Pauline will drown herself; so be it]. In fact, the Pauline that Charrière created is a far cry from the sad but beautiful descendants of Ophelia. When Fonbrune states that Pauline is in love with him, he does so by explaining that because she *cannot* see herself as a character in a novel, she does not realize she is in love (469). As for what she becomes, it must be considered one of the most audacious representations of a woman in eighteenth-century French fiction. In the conclusion to the novel, a letter from a servant reports that Pauline has safely escaped from France. To do so, she disguised herself as a man, an action her mother refused to take. The mother is recognized and detained while Pauline makes good her escape.[30] About halfway through the letter, it becomes a record of a conversation with Pauline. Thus Pauline ends *Lettres trouvées* and in such a way as to make Germaine, who began it, seem even more of a stereotype. The servant wants to know what to call her, but this audacious young woman has trouble answering him.

> Pauline tout court. Ni Madame ni Mademoiselle.... Mais qu'etes vous? je suis Mademoiselle, Mais j'aimerois mieux qu'on me crut Madame.... Disons donc Madame Pauline Madame Pauline ne va pas trop bien ... auriez vous dans votre famille quelque terre dont vous pussiez prendre le nom. Sans doute mais il ne nous est plus permis de porter de ces noms là. En Hollande cela n'a pas d'inconvenient.... [E]h bien donc je m'apellerai Madame Pauline de. non je ne puis m'y resoudre cela pouroit faire quelque tort à mes parens & deplaire à un homme à qui je veux toujours plaire. (482)

> [Just Pauline. Neither Mrs. nor Miss.... But which are you? I am "Miss" but I would prefer to be thought a "Mrs." Let us say, then, Mrs. Pauline. Mrs.

Pauline will not do very well. Would you have in your family some estate whose name you could take? No doubt, but it is no longer permitted to bear those names. In Holland there is no problem with that.... Very well, I will be called Mrs. Pauline of.... No, I cannot commit to it, it could harm in some way my relatives and displease a man whom I wish to always please.]

This novel about the Revolution concludes with a woman's search for an identity properly her own in the context of both the social flux then underway and of her desire to be named in such a way as to embody her choice of marital status. Such a conclusion illustrates the acuity with which *Lettres trouvées* raises the issue of woman's status.

The significance of Pauline may be confirmed if we consider her place in the narrative. With two exceptions, she is never spoken about but only to, and when spoken to she serves to disrupt a discussion between men. Her first appearance in the novel is representative of this. In a letter that Fonbrune writes to Alphonse about the war and politics, he digresses without warning into an apostrophe to "Beautiful Pauline," whom he has not yet even mentioned to Alphonse (421). This digression recurs on the following page and even interrupts his condemnation of counterrevolutionary armies: "Mais où m'entraîne mon saint patriotisme? Belle Pauline je vous oubliais" [But how far is my blessed patriotism taking me? Beautiful Pauline, I was forgetting you].[31] Pauline first appears in *Lettres trouvées*, then, as a figure serving to direct an epistolary exchange between men away from the Revolution and toward a woman. When words are attributed to Pauline we find they are not of the typically feminine variety. She speaks to warn Laurent in a skirmish that takes place inside the castle (465) and then to accept his marriage proposal, aggressively stipulating, however, that they must commit never to divorce (466).[32] This is not the stick figure/doll Germaine who was pictured sitting in her boudoir fantasizing about a letter.

Given a figure such as Pauline, it is not surprising to find that she serves to conclude the novel in a provocative way. In *Lettres trouvées,* we see represented first the stereotype of woman and then, in a more sketchy form, a radical new type of woman. As with Germaine, although the desired wedding is not set, it seems that it is not out of the heroine's reach. The text ends with Pauline only seeking, not finding, a new name, illustrating well the difficulty of representing female subjectivity in the novel of the eighteenth century. For the woman Charrière is outlining, even if the old names are set aside, there cannot yet be a name. There can only be an ellipsis: "Very well, I will be called Mrs. Pauline of...." It is as if Charrière, having come to focus on Pauline, could go no further in her analysis of this character. Given the framework of the epistolary novel, it would be logical to have Pauline become a letter writer at this point. As it stands, she never appears in this role.[33] Any incompleteness that we see in this text attests to its originality.[34] Pauline is an even more exceptional figure if we take into account the consistency with which Fauchery finds instead of such an unusual figure, the "eternal minor" punished time and time again for the sin of being woman.

The switch from one female protagonist to another effaces the stereotype represented by the first one, replacing it with the outline of a new image of woman. In the next text under consideration, a novel about the repatriation of the émigrés, the way in which the stereotype of woman served the purposes of oppression is manifest at a more profound level.

Questioning the Authority of Reading

Unlike Julie, Germaine, or Pauline, the heroine in *Sainte Anne* is not an aristocrat. She is the result of a liaison between a nobleman and the daughter of his gardener, a liaison he hastily legitimated before going off to war, where he was killed (9:267). What is most particular about Mlle d'Estival is that she is illiterate. The novel begins with, "Elle ne sait pas lire!" [She can't read!], and Charrière referred to *Sainte Anne* by that tag (257). At first glance it might seem that she is foregrounding this character's illiteracy in order to make a point about the way in which illiteracy (then affecting twice as many women as men) disempowers women. For example, in the case of novels featuring exotic heroines, Julia Douthwaite finds that "access to education and learned language form the central obstacles to [their] full participation in society."[35] In *Sainte Anne* we do not have an exotic heroine, and illiteracy functions differently. Mlle d'Estival's inability to read triggers a series of plot developments that will articulate a challenge to our ability to read. Charrière's innovation in this novel is more far reaching than in the novels previously considered.

As with "Le Noble" and *Lettres trouvées*, the plot here involves an obstacle to the union of two young lovers. In this instance, there is no disapproving father to overcome. The obstacle to their union is constituted in part by the heroine, who condemns the institution of marriage, and in part by a conspiracy to marry her off to a different man. The man she loves will have to propose twice before their marriage can take place. A comparison of the two scenes where she is shown responding to a proposal of marriage from him reveals how the illiteracy of the female protagonist is used to make a comment on our reading of the novel.

The man whom Mlle d'Estival loves is Sainte Anne, an émigré called home to France by his mother after the threat of the guillotine had passed. Setting the historical context for the novel, the details of his homecoming also evoke the passing of ancien régime society. The day Sainte Anne returned to his ancestral home, he found that his mother had assembled his female relatives. "Leurs peres, leurs maris, leurs fils avoient péri, ou vivoient encore dans cet exil auquel s'étoit condamné une partie de la noblesse françoise" (265) [Their fathers, their husbands, their sons had died, or lived still in that exile to which a part of the French nobility had condemned itself]. The noblewomen relentlessly recount to Sainte Anne lugubrious accounts of death and mayhem. Under these circumstances, the young nobleman falls in love with Mlle d'Estival, a woman who would have been, under the old social order, an unthinkable choice.

When Sainte Anne first proposes to Mlle d'Estival, she refuses him. This first proposal scene is striking because of the setting in which it occurs and the form Mlle d'Estival's refusal takes. Sainte Anne walks her home one night and takes a route past the cemetery. This setting results predictably enough in a formulaic description, including the fear of ghosts, the appearance of "petites flammes bleuâtres sortant de dessous terre" [little bluish flames coming out from underneath the ground], and the spooky hooting of owls, not to mention the fearfulness of the superstitious young girl, daunted by the proximity of those who are buried there (272). The dead in this scene are linked metonymically to the dead whose absence set the historical context for this novel. That the tutor of Sainte Anne is also buried in this graveyard, and that the young man stops kissing Mlle d'Estival when the voices of the dead cry out at his blasphemy, delimits the presence of patriarchal authority. It is no surprise that a union as improper as one between a nobleman and a gardener's granddaughter should not be furthered by what takes place in such a location. For the reader, this scene seems like a gothic cliché;

indeed, it is telegraphically summed up, in the words of one character, as "cet endroit lugubre cette fille craintive" (276) [that lugubrious place, that fearful girl].[36] The form of Mlle d'Estival's rejection of Sainte Anne's proposal creates a shocking contrast to the literary convention of the graveyard setting. Mlle d'Estival could have accepted Sainte Anne's proposal or at least turned him down in an appropriate feminine manner. Instead, she turns down the man she loves by systematically enumerating a catalogue of married couples she has known, including her parents, and analyzing the various ways that the institution of marriage made them unhappy (273–74). As it stands, this first proposal scene embodies the incompatibility between a scene (the spooky graveyard) whose meaning is given by a literary convention, and a social establishment for woman (marriage) whose meaning is given by Mlle d'Estival's all too realistic facts. With her perspicacious commentary on marriage, she debunks the myth that being a wife makes women happy. By so doing, her character exercises a right for which women had to fight: the right not to be married. However, the text articulates an even more radical statement about women when Mlle d'Estival finally does accept Sainte Anne's proposal. This may seem contradictory, since it would appear to endorse the myth that being a wife does make women happy. The implications of the second proposal scene, however, far exceed this myth.

A brief digression is in order before consideration of this second scene. In between the two proposals of marriage, a conspiracy is hatched that might preclude the desired marriage — a plot that serves to raise the issue of who has power over the seemingly autonomous young woman. Sainte Anne's mother absolutely disapproves of this young woman, and she conspires to marry off Mlle d'Estival to another man. For Mme de Sainte Anne, Mlle d'Estival threatens both her sense of family honor, representing the danger of a shocking union that "donneroit pour aïeul à mes petits-fils le jardinier de Monsieur d'Estival" (279) [would give my grandsons the gardener of Mr. d'Estival as ancestor], and her desire to have her son marry Mlle Rhedon, the daughter of the man that she wishes she had married after she became a widow (280). While Mlle Rhedon is delighted at the prospect, Sainte Anne adamantly opposes the arrangement, pointing out to his mother that Mlle Rhedon is as much the daughter of her mother as she is of her father. His mother is inflexible and resolute. Unfortunately, Mlle d'Estival represents such an improper match for a nobleman that he would have to be his own master (287) to manage it against the wishes of his sole surviving parent. Furthermore, the power Mme de Sainte Anne has over Mlle d'Estival is considerable. When Sainte Anne leaves to go visit one of their abandoned castles, his mother takes steps to force the young woman into a marriage with Sainte Anne's best friend, Tonquedec.

It is a letter and its reading that will set the stage for the second proposal scene, although this proposal will not be made by Sainte Anne. The scheme of Mme de Sainte Anne is halted at the very party celebrating the success of this scheme. All the characters, except Sainte Anne, are gathered for a dinner party in honor of Mlle d'Estival's imminent marriage to Tonquedec. However, Mme de Sainte Anne's jubilation at having prevented her son from marrying someone other than Mlle Rhedon is troubled by an incident suggesting the young people around her are not as much under her thumb as she had assumed. "Je m'apperçois, dit-elle, que personne n'a chez moi moins d'autorité que moi" (304) [I notice, she said, that no one has less authority in my house than I do]. Her pique is caused by the way in which a mysterious letter is handled. This letter is one that Mlle d'Estival pulls out of her purse while everyone is seated at the dinner table. Being illiterate, she cannot read it, and so she passes it on to Mlle Rhedon, her rival for Sainte Anne, asking her to read it. Mlle Rhedon reads the letter but then passes it on to Tonquedec, despite Mme de Sainte Anne's efforts to take possession of it. Tonquedec reads the letter but then passes on to Mlle d'Estival not the letter but the right to decide what it means. The letter is from Sainte Anne's manservant, and in it, he tells Mlle d'Estival that if she marries anyone other than his master, Sainte Anne will die. Both the readers of the letter, Mlle de Rhedon and Tonquedec, could have held the letter and used it to further their own desires: for Mlle de Rhedon, this would mean marriage to Sainte Anne; for Tonquedec, marriage to Mlle d'Estival. Both the readers choose to pass on the letter, causing Mlle d'Estival to receive her second marriage proposal indirectly from Sainte Anne. Right in front of Mme de Sainte Anne, Tonquedec asks Mlle d'Estival whether she prefers him or Sainte Anne (306). The young woman chooses Sainte Anne because she loves him. The sequence of readings that brings about the happy ending reflects a lateral, not hierarchical, power structure, so that mutual trust and sacrifice are the determining factors, not any sort of dominance.[37]

I have considered this scene with the manservant's letter as the second proposal scene in the novel, even though Sainte Anne is not present to do the proposing. His physical absence confirms the freedom that is given to the woman: the ability to choose her husband on her own. Furthermore, having the movement of the letter serve to redistribute the authority for who will dispose of Mlle d'Estival's hand in marriage provides a striking contrast with the first proposal scene. To appreciate the nature of this conclusion, we need only consider how Madame de Sainte Anne is dis- armed. The oppositional parent is reconciled to her son's marriage when one of the guests makes her read a letter from Sainte Anne in which he presents as a fact his attachment to Mlle d'Estival: "Mademoiselle de Kerber, en éclairant Madame de Ste. Anne, *l'avoit forcée* à souscrire de bonne grace à ce qu'elle ne pouvoit empêcher" (306; emphasis added) [Miss de Kerber, by enlightening Mrs. Sainte Anne, *had forced* her to endorse what she could not prevent]. The gothic graveyard scene, whose reading is predetermined, has vanished, to be replaced by a scene in which reading can contest the dominant power structure.

Once the d'Estival/Sainte Anne wedding is set, the other dinner guests manifest a fever for nuptials, and within the space of two pages no fewer than four marriages are set. Such a plethora of weddings in a conclusion, unless it is a comedy by Molière or Marivaux, seems out of place, and the narrator, anticipating some resistance on the part of the reader, intervenes at this point to defend the plausibility of the conclusion:

> C'est bien assez que les lectures soient inutiles; elles seroient très-nuisibles, si d'après de romanesques folies qui n'ont rien coûté à l'auteur, on sacrifioit des sentimens plus vrais, plus naturels, et qui sont parfaitement honnêtes. Laissons quelques admirateurs de Werther se tuer, et quelques folles pleurer toute leur vie ce qu'elles n'ont peut-être jamais eu sujet d'aimer. Il ne faut pas dans la vie véritable imiter un invraisemblable roman. (308)

> [It's already enough that reading is useless. It would be very harmful if, after novelistic flights of fancy that cost the author nothing, one sacrificed feelings that are more true, more natural, and in fact perfectly honest. Let a few admirers of Werther kill themselves, and a few madwomen cry their whole life over never perhaps having had a reason to love. One must not in real life imitate an unrealistic novel.]

It seems as if the narrator is defying the reader to find the wedding-prone characters of the conclusion deficient in feelings that are "true ... natural, and ... perfectly honest"; to find, in other words, that the conclusion is "unrealistic." And yet, the conclusion is precisely that.[38]

Faced with such a confrontation between a cliché that, in the context of this novel, is bound to seem *invraisemblable*, and an imperative from the narrator to accept the cliché as *vraisemblable*, the reader may be led to question this category. We know that this category has a repressive function: "What a particular society judges to be logical or probable is always bound up with a prior determination of what is deemed proper."[39] Charrière's conclusion contests what society deems proper by asking the question, Who is to say what is and is not *vraisemblable*?[40] Is it *invraisemblable* for a woman's freedom to choose her spouse to be coded as desirable by appending to it the many-happy-marriages conclusion, a literary sign for "All's well that ends well"? In provoking from us these questions, she recreates the act of reading inscribed in the route taken by the manservant's letter. Passing on the crucial letter, the fictional readers staged the question, Who will have power over Mlle d'Estival? Daring the reader to see an *invraisemblable* conclusion as *vraisemblable*, *Sainte Anne* stages the question, Who will have power over what is proper?

In the three novels considered here, there is a progression in Charrière's innovation with regard to the figure of the heroine. Undermining specific stereotypes of women leads finally to contesting the force of stereotyping itself, as expressed in the constraint of *vraisemblance*. In this, her fiction has a political content and possibly more. Hypothesizing that "an impotent feminine sensibility is a basic structure of the novel, representing one of the important ways that the novel embodies the basic structures of this society," Myra Jehlen proposes that "the achievement of female autonomy must have radical implications not only politically but also for the very forms and categories of all our thinking."[41] The heroines considered here are all the more distinctive because the auton-omy they attain is represented in a text which itself challenges ways of thinking about women. Their distinctiveness is well illustrated in a novel of which we have only one sentence, *Camille ou le nouveau roman* (1796). Through this novel, she proposed to create a radically new hero-ine: "Mon plan ... a été de changer ce que les romans font toujours c'est de faire l'heroine belle comme le jour, je la ferai ici laide comme la nuit" (9:355) [My plan ... was to change what novels always do: namely, to make the heroine as pretty as a picture. Here I will make her as ugly as sin]. In fact, Charrière did create such a radically new heroine: her names are Julie, Germaine/Pauline, and Mlle d'Estival.

2
The Doomed Heroine:
The Impasse of Revolutionary Ideology

Charrière's heroines function at two different levels. On the one hand, in the three feminocentric novels discussed so far, each progresses toward a successful resolution of the conflict set up by the plot. On the other hand, these novels themselves question at a more general level the authority of literary conventions that reduce women to stereotypes.

A much more powerful reductionism was in force during the course of the gendering of the new social order after the French Revolution. Women, first targeted as a source of what had gone wrong with the ancien régime, were eventually reconfigured as positive images for the new republic. No longer the insidious corrupters of men in public office, women were perceived relative to the model of the modest, faithful wife who stayed at home, breastfeeding the future citizens of the new republic. How would an author like Charrière represent the force of this new image? We have seen that in *Lettres trouvées*, a novel set in 1793, she created a heroine so unconventional that even naming her was impossible. However, the oppositional parent, Germaine/Pauline's father, was presented as a man firmly fixed in the social order. Regardless of who wins the war, the Marquis de *** has no doubts about where he belongs. In contrast, when the oppositional parent confronted by the heroine is a man seeking an identity in the social flux triggered by the Revolution, the heroine is doomed.

To consider Charrière's fictional representation of this political transformation, we must first confront a paradox. Judging from her fiction, she is capable of articulating a perspicacious analysis of woman's social status. In addition, during the revolutionary period, she was singularly privileged by her situation. Charrière had the luxury of being able to publish, and of doing so at her own expense. During the Terror, when women in France were exiled and executed, she had the freedom, from her location outside the country, to proclaim a political opposition to all parties. In texts such as "Lettre d'un évêque français à la nation" (1789), "Lettres trouvées dans la neige" (1793), and "De l'esprit et des rois" (1798), she generously damns revolutionaries and counterrevolutionaries alike for the weaknesses of their political philosophy and the excesses of their military campaigns. Antagonizing the various political factions was no problem for Charrière, tucked away as she was outside of France. Given the novels she wrote, one might have expected on her part an articulate demand for social justice for women in her various suggestions for redressing the inequities of French society. However, with the single exception of the fragmentary "Lettre d'un Anglois à un député de l'Assemblée nationale de France" (1790[?]), nowhere in the reforms she proposes do women's rights appear. The poor, the clergy, the aristocracy, all have a stake; only women are omitted. It would be difficult to assume she thought that the reforms she advocated would, if implemented, benefit men and women equally, for she had a clear understanding of the difference between the rules that determined the status of men and those that determined that of women. In *Lettres écrites de Lausanne*, a mother explains to her daughter the difference between virtue for men and women, to which her daughter responds:

> Mais, maman, les hommes n'ont-ils pas reçu les mêmes loix; pourquoi se permettent-ils d'y manquer, & de nous en rendre l'observation difficile? — Je ne saurois trop, Cécile, que vous répondre; mais cela ne nous regarde pas. Je n'ai point de fils. (8:160–61)

> [But, Mother, didn't men receive the same laws? Why do they allow themselves to disregard them and to make respecting these laws difficult for us? I cannot think how to answer you, Cécile, but it does not concern us. I have no son.]

In the mother's dismissal of the question raised by her daughter we recognize Charrière's reluctance to put forth gross generalities as an explanation for complex problems, as well as her sense of the different rules that applied to women and those that applied to men.

In her ideas for improving society, Charrière was not unaware that these would have different implications for women and men. Why, then, do her political works omit any consideration of women? Charrière might have felt that the political transformation underway, which she viewed with considerable cynicism, left so little hope for social justice for either the people or the aristocracy, that even to mention the special case of the status of women in the context of this political change was pointless. She was a confirmed skeptic. In a letter written to her friend Henriette L'Hardy during the difficult period of August 1793, Charrière reflected upon revolutions, saying "il m'est impossible de trouver fort à redire aux revolutions" [I find it impossible to blame revolutions out of hand]. She offers the metaphor of the world as a big fellow with a game leg who limps "tantot à droite tantot à gauche" (4:161) [sometimes to the right sometimes to the left], so that monarchies and republics come and go with a predictable monotony. If not dictated by her skepticism, Charrière's omission of women from her proposals for social reform nonetheless seems puzzling if we study the one text in which she does address the issue of women's rights. "Lettre d'un Anglois" is only three pages long, but the text presents one of the most stark and succinct statements of women's equality to men. It is difficult to assess this text, however, because it is a satire. In "Lettre d'un Anglois," an Englishman complains about the unfortunate effect that a revolution among the horses over in France has had on the horses across the Channel. The English horses have already begun agitating, and some of them have gone so far as to undertake a work slowdown. He fears they will, in turn, inspire the English ladies to revolt. That the text is satirical leaves uncertain the question of whether she was advocating women's rights or not.

> Ce coup de collier de la populace des Chevaux a donné à penser à nos Dames; elles ne voient pas pourquoi aucune déclaration de droits n'a encore prononcé leur égalité avec nous à moins que *tous les hommes ne naissent egaux* ne veuille dire *toutes les creatures humaines naissent egales.* (10:317; emphasis in the original)

> [This shrugging off of the shackles by the horse population has gotten our ladies thinking. They do not see why a declaration of rights has not yet asserted their equality with us, unless *all men are born equal* means *all human creatures are born equal.*]

Up to this point, the philosophy is consistent with Charrière's profound sense of human equality, but it does not end here. The Englishman goes on to express his concern that the ladies, not satisfied with mere theory, will next want to vote, if not run for office. As Charrière tended to depreciate extreme measures of any type, the last clause giving women not just rights but the vote and the eligibility to run for any public office whatsoever, may well be intended to be rejected by the reader as unreasonable. (Indeed, the idea of allowing uneducated women to vote caused many educated women to recoil.) Despite the lack of political commentary on women in her political writings, an astute representation of what the Revolution meant for Frenchwomen may be inferred from her representation of the Revolution in fiction.[1]

Marie-Claire Vallois has argued persuasively that the image of women in two French novels, Bernadin de Saint-Pierre's *Paul et Virginie* (1787) and François-René de Chateaubriand's *Atala, ou les amours de deux sauvages dans le désert* (1801), illustrates the social change brought about by the French Revolution, with its attendant distinction between man and woman. She refers to a "*supplément* of history of the revolutionary happening" located between these two novels, each of which features a dramatic burial scene that lays the heroine to rest.[2] According to Vallois, this burial symbolizes the real exclusion of women from the body politic in consequence not just of laws that were passed but of the new domesticity taking root. Similarly, in Carole Pateman's revisionist history of the social contract, she points out that "the story of the original contract tells of the genesis of a society that is structured into two spheres — although we are usually told only half the story and so we only hear about the origin of the public 'universal' sphere."[3] Charrière's *Henriette et Richard* (1792/3), a novel clearly marked by the turmoil of the Revolution, can fill the space between *Paul et Virginie* and *Atala*, and it can tell the other half of the story through its depiction of what happened to woman during the Revolution, showing the construction of the private sphere at work. Building on what was the standard eighteenth-century plot of a heroine whose father opposes her choice of spouse, Charrière integrated into it the effects of the new, gendered bourgeois politics, and created a novel structured by the impasse that had been set up for women.[4] Although Henriette does not die, there can be no successful resolution to the conflict pitting her against an oppositional father. That this is indeed the case emerges forcefully from a comparison of Henriette with two other heroines plotted in the context of the Revolution: Victorine in the play *La Parfaite liberté (ou les vous et les toi)* (1794) and Honorine in the novel *Honorine d'Userche* (1795/6), a novel published in a 1798 collection (*Trois femmes*) under the pseudonym of the Abbé de la Tour. Charrière's Honorine of October 1788, like her Henriette of December 1788, is destined to be unsatisfied because man's need to situate himself in the emerging social order constitutes an impasse for woman's desire. Victorine in *La Parfaite liberté* escapes this impasse only because the man who poses an obstacle to her desire, her guardian, feels well established, just as Germaine/Pauline's father did.

Henriette et Richard was for a long time considered fragmentary, but as the editors of the *Œuvres complètes* point out, the missing pieces do not preclude a legitimate reading (8:271). What is still disconcerting is the form of this novel. *Henriette et Richard* is recounted primarily by an omniscient narrator who makes, at times, metadiscursive comments, such as, "Il faut reprendre les choses d'un peu plus haut" (367) [We must begin with matters even earlier than this]. This narrative style is more prevalent in the nineteenth century, however, than in the eighteenth, and is uncommon for a woman author.[5] But in addition to the use of the omniscient narrator, Charrière's novel presents a blend of narrative styles. While the interpolation of letters in the narrative is not particularly problematic, the occasional emergence of first person pronouns, in the absence of any explanation of who such a first-person narrator might be, is.[6] What to make of the following identification?

> Que je sois le mari le fils, la fille, le domestique de la Tante d'Henriette ou cette tante elle même toujours est-il certain que je ne suis pas gentilhomme, & de plus je proteste n'avoir encore rien perdu à la revolution. (304)

> [That I be the husband, the son, the daughter, the servant of Henriette's aunt or this aunt, still it is certain that I am not a gentleman and furthermore I proclaim that I lost nothing so far in the Revolution.]

The status of these first-person pronouns is difficult to reconcile with the metadiscursive comments made by the third-person narrator.[7] In Charrière's most negative feminocentric novel, the narrative voice through which the heroine will be presented is characterized by ambivalence, vacillating between the authority proper to a first-person narrator and that proper to a third-person narrator, as if it were difficult to authorize the fate being prepared for her.

The plot of the novel resembles those discussed in chapter 1 to the extent that it involves a father's obstinate opposition to his daughter's choice of spouse. This opposition is derived from family history, and in fact it predates the love between the two young lovers. Thus, the early part of the novel must trace the life of Henriette's father, Henri Giroud, and of Richard's mother, Genevieve des Echelles. Although, in principle, Henri and Genevieve could marry each other, they do not: he wants her, but she does not want him. This possibility of marriage fuels Henri's obstinacy in holding out for her hand. Raised by a modest man who became wealthy through his own hard work, Henri differs from his father because he disdains being a kindly landowner and he longs to rise above what he considers to be his mediocre rank (288). Unfortunately for him, even his aspiration to join the military is inhibited by his lack of social status. As a consolation prize, he decides to marry Genevieve de Larche, a poor but aristocratic woman. Henri persuades his father to sound out her father concerning this marriage, but when the two fathers talk to Genevieve, they make a discovery that causes Henri's lifelong humiliation. Genevieve explains to them that she must decline the marriage offer because Henri has put a local girl in the cruelest of dilemmas (291). Horrified at what his son has done, Henri's father makes out his will so as to take care of everyone (including the pregnant girl and her baby), gives some of his late wife's jewels to Genevieve, and then dies.

Henri and Genevieve go on to marry someone else of their own class, they each have a child (he has a daughter named Henriette, she has a son named, less egotistically, Richard), and are eventually widowed. In this time, Henri never forgets Genevieve and his humiliation. Henri arranges for his own tutor, the Abbé des Rois, to come and educate Henriette, and when the tutor arrives, he brings Richard, Genevieve's son, because Richard is also his pupil. The meeting is pleasurable for the two children and for the tutor but not for poor Henri, who sees only the past and with it his own humiliation. Henriette and Richard are raised in close proximity to each other and soon fall in love. While the Abbé des Rois would be happy to see his two pupils wed, Henriette's father places an obstacle in the way of this union: unless Genevieve marries Henri, Henri will not permit his daughter to marry her son. Because Genevieve states point blank that she will never agree to marry Henri, and he makes it equally clear that he will never lift this restriction, the marriage between Henriette and Richard seems impossible. In contrast to the novels previously considered, *Henriette et Richard* ends without the obstacle to the desire of the female protagonist having been overcome.

Given that the heroines previously considered managed to marry the man of their choice, might it be possible to imagine a happy conclusion to this novel? We have seen that in the case of *Lettres trouvées dans des porte-feuilles*, set like *Henriette et Richard* in the context of political events, both Germaine and Pauline seemed headed for the man of their choice. The context of *Henriette et Richard*, however, is tied much more directly to the Revolution. While *Lettres trouvées* opened onto the world of postrevolutionary turmoil, *Henriette et Richard* remains firmly marked by the context of the Revolution. Instead of the social scene in London with the idle émigrés and the battlegrounds out in the French countryside, the action takes place in Paris, and Henriette's first letter to Richard, in which she bemoans her father's opposition to their marriage, bears a telling date: 29 December 1788. Two descriptions, one of a scene in which Richard saves Henri from the threats of the mob, and one where a fleeing duchess arrogantly borrows money from him, reinforce the intrusion of political events on private affairs. But the most significant difference between *Lettres trouvées* and *Henriette et Richard* is the difference between the two oppositional fathers. The father of Germaine/Pauline is secure in his status even without knowing whether his side will or will not prevail, whereas Henriette's father is working out a new identity for himself in the context of the social transformation underway. This novel reflects the gendering of the new bourgeois individual as male so well that there is no possible hope for woman. Unlike Germaine/Pauline, Henriette is doomed.

In assessing the role of revolutionary ideology and the way in which it is a determining factor in the heroine's fate, it is necessary to identify the type of obstacles she encounters. Henriette confronts two different female character types that none of the heroines previously considered faced. What is striking about these characters is that the two different misogynistic images of woman they represent is particularly charged during the revolutionary period: woman as embodied in the unnatural and evil aristocrat and woman viewed as a sexually unbridled being. Of equal significance is the depiction of Henriette's father as the emerging bourgeois individual and the way in which this identity creates an obstacle for Henriette greater than that faced by Julie, Germaine/Pauline, and Mlle d'Estival.

Woman as the Unnatural and Evil Aristocrat

> MADAME DE V ALINE: "Un charme invincible auquel feu son mari a
> seul resisté lui donne cet ascendant." (406)
> [An invincible charm which her late husband alone resisted gives her
> this ascendancy.]

The Revolution represented in part an expression of anger against not just the upper classes but the women of the upper classes and the power they held. Even Olympe de Gouges, in her "Déclaration des droits de la femme" [Declaration of the rights of women] (1791), addresses words of reproach to women in power:

> Les femmes ont fait plus de mal que de bien. La contrainte et la dissimulation ont été leur partage. Ce que la force leur avait ravi, la ruse leur a rendu.... elles commandaient au crime comme à la vertu. Le gouvernement français, surtout, a dépendu, pendant des siècles, de l'administration nocturne des femmes.

> [Women have done more harm than good. Restraint and dissimulation have been their province. What force had seized from them, cunning gave back to them.... They directed crime as well as virtue. The French government, especially, has depended for centuries on the nocturnal governance of women.][8]

The image of aristocratic women came to be tainted by the association between them and power, resulting in a perception of aristocratic women as ruthless, even demonic.[9] This misogynistic perspective on women emerges in *Henriette et Richard* through what is a standard plot development in novels, where the heroine struggles to marry the man she loves: one way for the author to put an obstacle in her way is to incorporate a character who plots to marry her off to someone else. Although "Le Noble" does not feature this obstacle, both *Lettres trouvées* and *Sainte Anne* do. Between these two novels on the one hand, and *Henriette et Richard* on the other, the characters who are responsible for this obstacle differ considerably.

In *Lettres trouvées,* Germaine confronted a plot on the part of her guardian duchess to marry her off to someone else. This aristocratic woman is presented as foolish, not vicious, and when Germaine uncovers the alternative marriage plot, she is able to embarrass the duchess: "Je l'ai si fixément regardée, qu'elle a rougi & n'a pu continuer" (8:427) [I stared at her so fixedly that she blushed and could not continue]. The decoy marriage plot in *Sainte Anne*, concocted and aggressively pursued by the mother of Sainte Anne, came closer to happening. This aristocratic woman, however, is not presented as evil or unnatural. Instead, the comparison of her to Mlle d'Estival's own low-born mother serves to make of them two examples of the same type: the domineering mother.

> Les deux meres avoient beaucoup fait, l'une pour son fils, l'autre pour sa fille, et vouloient actuellement s'en récompenser beaucoup, se servant pour cela de l'objet de leurs soins, de maniere à faire douter si elles n'avoient pas eu toujours plus d'égoïsme que de tendresse. (9:297)

> [The two mothers had done much, the one for her son, the other for her daughter, and wanted now to reward themselves thoroughly for it, using the object of their care in order to do so, and in such a way as to make it doubtful whether they had not always had more egoism than tenderness.][10]

Madame de Sainte Anne is not inherently evil, and she is not all-powerful. Her son is aware, if only tentatively so, of the "bornes de l'autorité d'une mere" [limits to the authority of a mother] and, as we have seen, the plotting of this aristocratic woman can be disarmed by her son's young friends. Setting up a sharp contrast to Germaine's meddling duchess and Mlle d'Estival's reluctant mother-in-law-to-be, Henriette's obstacle will be contrived by the archetype of the evil aristocratic woman. Through this character, a point of intensity emerges from the novel most closely linked to the Revolution.

Before Henriette faces this evil woman, she faces another character who would marry her off to someone besides Richard. Significantly, the first plotter, the father of the little marquis de Loisel, is male. A slight, negative quality is attributed to his image when he is described as being "de mauvaise humeur" (8:328) [in a bad mood] upon finding that his scheme to acquire Henriette for his son is not going to have smooth sailing, and this negative quality is reinforced by his willingness to slander her beloved tutor (327) in order to carry out his plan.[11] The comte de Loisel's plot to marry Henriette to his son can threaten her, but it is because of her father's power over her, not because of Loisel's evil character. After turning down categorically an offer, Henriette writes: "Je crains [que mon père] ne me donne plus de Choix qu'entre le Marquis de

Loisel et un Couvent" (339) [I fear (that my father) will no longer give me any choice except that between the Marquis de Loisel and a convent]. Furthermore, the power of Henriette's father to second Loisel's scheme is limited: he can stop a marriage, not force one to take place. All in all, the danger posed by the comte de Loisel's plot to marry off Henriette to someone other than Richard is not overwhelming. Certainly his negative qualities pale in comparison to those of the second plotter.

This second plotter is female and vile; she is unlike any characters we have seen in the other novels. Neither a foolish noblewoman nor a domineering mother, Madame de Valine is presented as the archetype of the vicious aristocratic woman: precisely what the revolutionaries were targeting. Indeed, "Valine" is perhaps meant to be read as "vilaine" [nasty], except that the adjective hardly does her justice. This is evident in the life story given to her, which emphasizes her lack of natural female virtue. Madame de Valine's unnaturally close social relationship to her brother takes the place of her role as wife to her husband.[12] Her husband lets her do as she pleases, except what would have ruined the family. He pays her an allowance to care for their daughter but has put their son out of her demonic clutches by having the boy raised abroad. His father "avoit pensé devoir mettre l'ocean entre [son fils] & les seductions de sa mere" [had felt it best to put an ocean between (his son) and the seductions of his mother].[13] In the life story Charrière imagined for Madame de Valine, we can see the negative image of woman that will be countered by soon-to-be enforced maternalism and later by principles in the Napoleonic Code.

Madame de Valine's scheme to have her brother marry Henriette is more menacing than that of Loisel because she makes use not only of the power of Henriette's father but of her own immoral ruthlessness. Every time her plot meets a snag, she rethinks it and forges ahead. She even succeeds in changing Henriette's name, persuading Henriette's father to rename his daughter after a bit of land he bought upon the advice of Madame de Valine (400). *Henriette et Richard* has no formal conclusion but ends with the description of Madame de Valine's life story and of her ongoing efforts to arrange for her brother to marry Henriette. It is as if the agency of revolutionary-period heroines is profoundly diminished once the character of the evil aristocratic woman has been established.

Furies

FREDERICA AND HANNA: "Les deux Megeres s'obstinent à demeurer,
à s'injuriér on ne savoit trop en quelle Langue, de maniere à arreter
les promeneurs qui a la fin en firent justice." (309–10)
[The two furies obstinately remained, swearing at each other in some
incomprehensible language, in such a way as to halt passersby who in
the end gave them what they deserved.]

Not only aristocratic women were the target of revolutionary misogyny in France. Throughout the history of women's education, women had been viewed as excessively sexual beings whose education had to serve as a brake on this characteristic.[14] However, revolutionary ideology presents a more extreme case. Politically active women were presented as crazed sexual beings. Whereas in the novels previously considered, woman's sexual desire has not been explicitly presented (with the possible exception of Julie and Valaincourt kissing in the darkened hallway), in *Henriette et Richard* it will be. Henriette has two servant girls, Frederica and Hanna, who hate each other and one of them forces Henriette to walk in on the other girl with her lover. Henriette describes how she was taken by Frederica, "souriant comme je pense qu'on sourit en Enfer" [smiling as I believe one smiles in hell], to Hanna's room: "Dieu quelle scene!" [Lord, what a scene!]. Not content with having shocked her young mistress, Frederica, "la Furie" [the fury], "l'infernale italienne" [the infernal Italian], tried to drag Henriette into her father's office to tell what she had witnessed (311). Unwilling to get the two servants fired, Henriette retains from this experience a fear of them. Her trusty manservant, Lambert, must sleep in the next room so he can rescue her if she screams. Even after her father replaces Frederica and Hanna, Henriette cannot forget them. She tells Richard:

[Elles] me laisserent des souvenirs, des réflexions, des avertissemens qui ne m'ont jamais quittée. J'avois vû des passions dont je sentois que je ne me garantirois pas toujours et dont je pouvois être la victime. Oui la malheureuse victime ... mais voila tout ce que je puis être, car mon horreur pour ce que jai vû, s'est conservée telle jusqu'à ce jour qu'il n'est pas possible que je tombe dans un semblable désordre. (313)

[They left me with memories, thoughts, warnings that have never left me. I had seen passions that I felt I could not always guard against, and of which I could become victim. Yes, the unhappy victim ... but that is all I can be,

because my horror for what I saw has been so well preserved to this day that
it is not possible I should fall into a similar disorder.]

On the one hand, Henriette's sexual initiation instills in her the "pudeur"
(a sense of shame) that was being required of women to preclude them
from falling into the sexual excesses that were so feared. The narrator's
intervention reinforces this element of conservatism: "Ici notre Héroïne
surprise elle même des paroles qu'elle venoit de prononcer, s'arrête, et
sourit" [Here, our heroine, surprised herself at the words she had just
said, stops and smiles]. On the other hand, it also gives her knowledge of
her own sexual desire, a desire that can never be satisfied unless her
father relents and lets her marry Richard.[15] *Henriette et Richard*
confirms in a graphic manner Outram's view that "the eighteenth-century
novel, particularly after Rousseau, implied all the Revolution's obsessive
connection between the history of the heroines' bodies and the nature of
the public order itself."[16] In Charrière's most negative novel about
women such a connection is manifested in the awakening of Henriette's
sexual desire after her exposure to the two furies.

The Bourgeois Individual

> HENRIETTE TO RICHARD: "Ne sommes nous pas
> l'Un comme l'Autre?" (310)
> [Are we not the one like the other?]

The female figures of the evil aristocratic powermonger and the fury
represent what was attacked by revolutionary ideology. Simultaneously,
what was being validated was a gendered society where man would be
the bourgeois individual and woman the homebound spouse and mother.
Gutwirth explains that "in the long-begun political struggle for greater
individual autonomy, men were being driven toward all the forms of self-
realization, including the sexual, yet all the while needing to contain, or
recontain, these same drives among women."[17] Such a search for self-
realization describes with accuracy the figure of Henri Giroud, especially
if he is compared to the oppositional fathers previously mentioned. This
patriarch is not an aristocrat, but his qualities as a man are privileged,
endowing this character with an attribute we have not yet seen in these
other fathers, namely personal desire.

The heroines considered in chapter 1 had to fight a typical ancien régime parent whose opposition to their choice of spouse was based on the effort to enforce and perpetuate a class hierarchy privileging nobility. The father in "Le Noble," attached to the nobility through blind devotion, explicitly charges his daughter with betraying "moi, & ... mes Ayeux" (8:28) [me and my ancestors], and the understanding father in *Lettres trouvées*, attached to the nobility on moral grounds, analyzes his daughter's misconduct in more specific terms. He states that for her to have written to Alphonse was an act of disobedience against her father (8:451). In contrast, *Sainte Anne* featured opposition from a female parent — Sainte Anne's mother. She added to the objection based on social issues (the wish that her grandchildren not have a gardener for ancestor) a preference based on personal issues: regret over the marriage that she did not make. Because of the personal component, Henri's objection to his daughter's choice of spouse is most similar to this last one. (We must nonetheless bear in mind that as a father he has more power than Madame de Sainte Anne.) This element of personal desire on the part of the father distinguishes *Henriette et Richard* from the other novels. Henri opposes Henriette's choice not because of class-based objections to the prospective in-law but because of his personal desire to marry Genevieve. He is not an aristocrat, but he is a patriarch. In addition, he poses a more serious threat to the heroine because he is the bourgeois individual. Once Henri has attached the "I want Genevieve" clause to Henriette's permission to marry, her efforts to marry Richard will be doomed to failure unless her father gets the girl of his dreams. By basing the father's opposition to his daughter's choice of spouse on his personal desire rather than on aristocratic prejudice, Charrière succeeds in writing into her history of the French Revolution what the Revolution effaced: the constitution of man by the erasure of woman.

That Henri is delimited as the emerging bourgeois individual becomes evident at the point in the plot where the Revolution erupts and touches both Henri and Henriette, albeit in different ways. This eruption takes place at a moment when the conflict between the two of them over her desire to marry Richard has reached an extreme degree of intensity. One morning Henriette awakens to find that her father has left Paris. We also learn that Henri, like Molière's Orgon, has some compromising papers in his house. The difference between Henriette and her father that is worked out in the course of this plot development is set up first of all in terms of space. Henri not only flees Paris, he goes to the countryside and satisfies his longing for Genevieve at least partially by buying her castle. In contrast, Henriette remains in the private space of the house following her father's orders, and may have to face the mob all by herself. Thus Henri's wish to make an inconspicuous departure from the city leads him to sacrifice his daughter's security to his own security, his desires as an individual having taken priority over his paternal role and any concern he might have over seeing to it that she remain a virgin. Henriette stays behind in the confines of the house, from there eventually moving into a convent. Although the move into the convent is meant to ensure her physical safety, the transit from house to convent is a woman's version of the man's transit from house to countryside. What happens with the compromising papers Henri left behind in Henriette's care further differentiates them.

Henri leaves his daughter a letter of instructions concerning these papers, and his orders represent the axis around which the gendered ideology of the Revolution will imprint on the plot a distinction between man and woman not seen in novels previously discussed. In sum, Henri will make of his daughter the means to secure his own status in the new social order, using her as indiscriminately as he would any other person or object at his disposal. He instructs Henriette to hide the package containing the letters under her bed. He specifies that he prefers they not be destroyed, but in an emergency she is authorized either to give the package to M** or else to go ahead and destroy it (356). The documents become a problem after a group of men enters the house and searches it. Unable to find the package of documents because Henriette has slipped them into her skirt, they are leaving. Unfortunately, at the last minute one of the men remarks that regardless of whether Henriette is "femme ou fille" [woman or girl] she seems to be pregnant (358). Another man makes the obvious inference, "Si elle est grosse ... c'est des papiers de son pere" [If she is pregnant ... it is with her father's papers]. In fact, Henriette is heavy with not only her father's papers but with his status in the new social order. She protects his new status at home in their house while he protects his physical safety out in the countryside.

Alarmed by this close call, she writes to her father for further instructions, and they exchange letters concerning what is to be done with the documents. The contrast between these letters is of paramount importance. Her letter consists of two equal sections. In the first, she

explains what happened and asks that he choose between the two options
he had outlined in his first letter of instructions: "Ayez ... la bonté de me
repondre par l'un de ces [mots] *confiance* ou *neant*" (359) [Have ... the
kindness to answer me with one of these (words): *trust* or *nothingness*],
by which she requests him to tell her to choose between trusting M**
with the documents or dispatching them into nothingness. In the second
section of her letter she addresses the conflict existing between her father
and herself. Henriette's letter clearly separates the two issues of her
father's documents and of her own choice of spouse. The answer to
Henriette's letter is a curious text, integrating these two issues to such a
degree that the letter seems unfocused. Henri's answer is structured by
the recurrence of the word "trust" in answer to her query; it appears at
three different points (364–65). The space between the occurrences of
this word is taken up in first place by a disquisition on marriage; in
second place by an assertion of his authority over Henriette; and in third
place by a quick hint at what the documents are. This structure integrates
the issue of what to do with his documents with the issue of her desire to
marry Richard, and in this structure we may discern the contours of the
new bourgeois individual. He defines marriage as a social institution: "*La
nature* commande le penchant d'un sexe pour l'autre la société a tiré parti
de ce penchant pour s'organiser avec plus de stabilité" (364; emphasis
added) [*Nature* dictating the penchant of one sex for the other, society
has taken advantage of this penchant to organize itself with greater
stability]. By the terms of this argument, nature designed women to bear
children and to breastfeed them, and so women serve society better by
confining themselves to these duties. He defines his authority over his
daughter as absolute: "Il ne tient qu'à moi d'ordonner" [All I have to do
is give you an order], echoing a father's power over a daughter. Finally,
he reveals why he wants Henriette to give the documents to M** rather
than destroy them (an action that would entail less danger for her). As
was the case with his decision to flee Paris and to leave Henriette behind,
Henri risks his daughter's safety in order to guarantee his own status.
Henri asserts that although "les noms les objets peuvent y deplaire" [the
names, the items in them, may displease], what matters the most is that
the papers contain "la justification de la personne soupconnée" [the
justification of the person under suspicion] — namely, Henri. It is for this
reason that Henriette must act as a go-between for these two men, taking
documents on behalf of the one to the other. This means that when the

armed men who enter the house perceive Henriette as pregnant "with her father's papers," the apparent "child" that she is carrying is the justification of her father, or, in other words, his right of entry into the new social order. Reducing her to what can be sacrificed to ensure this status, he assigns primary importance to himself in his anxiety for a foothold in the emerging order. Henri's gesture parallels the larger political movement through which all men were being created equal at the same time that women in France were being legally and morally disempowered.[18]

Comparing the letters that Henriette and her father exchange, we see from Henri's missive that what matters to him is his own status, and that this takes priority over any role he might play in arranging to marry off his only child. Thus he retains the element of patriarchal authority and acquires, in addition, the force of the new ideology by the terms of which woman was to be naturally confined to the private sphere — a potent brew indeed. In contrast, the careful distinction in Henriette's letter between the two issues (her father's documents and her own desire) represents the effort to differentiate Henri's identity from her own fate, to be an individual herself. Henri counters her effort; when he departs/flees from Paris, he states that he is leaving "une fille ingratte qui meconnoit tous ses devoirs & paris où le peuple egaré ne distingue plus ses amis de ses oppresseurs" (356) [an ungrateful daughter who completely fails to understand her duty, and Paris where the confused people no longer distinguish their friends from their oppressors]. Henri conflates Henriette's failure to recognize his authority over her with the new society's delay in recognizing him as a valid member.

Henriette, Victorine, and Honorine

In *Henriette et Richard,* Charrière created an insurmountable impasse for her protagonist, as manifest not just in the obstacles she faces but also in her options. An elopement such as Julie undertook in "Le Noble" seems implausible, since Henriette is more conservative than Julie.[19] Might Henriette's father have a change of heart, as the Marquis de *** did in *Lettres trouvées dans des porte-feuilles*? Henri's repeated insistence that unless Genevieve agrees to marry him he will not permit Henriette to marry Richard makes this equally implausible. In fact, Henri goes so far as to lie point blank to his daughter, telling her that Richard had not saved him but had abandoned him to the mob — in an effort to blacken the man she loves (351). Might a friend such as l'abbé des Rois help to solve Henriette's problem as Tonquedec did in *Sainte Anne*? Because of the history and the nature of Henri's desire, receiving the help of a friend is not an option for Henriette. Indeed, the abbé may not be a good ally for Henriette, even though he favors her relationship with Richard. The problem is that the abbé des Rois can take steps to protect Genevieve from being forced to marry Henri, and what protects Genevieve makes her more unattainable. The more unattainable she becomes, the more Henri holds to his "deux Mariages, ou pas un" [two marriages or none] rule. His desire, based on an original humiliation, will always stand in the way of his daughter's desire.

With her creation of Henri Giroud, the emerging bourgeois individual, Charrière represented the one figure who could constitute an absolute obstacle to the desire of her protagonist, as evident in the conclusion to *Henriette et Richard*. All the main characters except Henriette have migrated to the countryside where Genevieve's castle (now Henri's) is situated. Meanwhile, all alone in Paris, Henriette is bereft of both father and lover. She has given up writing love letters to Richard (344), and she is unhappy (388).[20] Because it is more proper, she writes jointly to the abbé and Richard (392). In the last sentence of the novel, her unexpected arrival at the castle is noted as well as the fact that the first nobleman to be hanged has been executed.[21] The text, then, ends with no clue as to how Henriette might manage to marry the man of her choice — reasonably so, since there can be no solution to her dilemma. That Henriette is stymied may be confirmed if we consider two other texts by Charrière set in the context of the Revolution: *La Parfaite liberté (ou les vous et les toi)* and *Honorine d'Userche*. What pertains in this comparison is the nature of the character who opposes the heroine's choice of spouse. Victorine will confront a guardian who has already established his place in the postrevolutionary order, while Honorine will attempt to negotiate with a lover/brother who is unsettled by this order. Unlike Henriette, the female protagonist in *La Parfaite liberté* does marry the man of her choice, but the one in the novel will be foiled, just as Henriette was. While there is a difference in genre here, it is less significant than the way in which revolutionary ideology is inscribed on each text.

The plot of *La Parfaite liberté* is even more similar to Moliere's *Tartuffe* than is *Henriette et Richard* because not only are there incriminating documents in the house but the oppositional father is under the influence of a hypocrite. The difference between the two plots lies in the basis on which the would-be husband is rejected. Henri is opposed to Richard because Henri wants something for himself. In *La Parfaite liberté*, the young girl's guardian, Citizen Francoeur, is opposed to Victorine's choice of spouse not because of what he wants for himself but because the young man is of noble blood. Francoeur worries that his dearly beloved ward will not be happy married to a member of the defeated class. It is out of love for her that he contests her choice:

> Je l'aime trop pour l'exposer aux suites d'un pareil mariage ... Si le vieil homme aristocrate ressuscitoit chez cet aimable jeune homme, s'il l'entrainoit à des fautes à des malheurs [comme] nous en avons tant vus quel seroit le sort de cette pauvre [fille]! (7:398)

> [I love her too much to expose her to the consequences of such a marriage.... What if the old aristocrat resuscitated in this likeable young man, what if he dragged her into sins, into tragedies such as we have seen so often! What would be the fate of this poor (girl)!]

The old class distinction between the aristocracy and the lower classes, although responsible for many deaths during the Terror, is not what will pose a special problem for women during France's move away from an absolute monarchy. Thus, it is possible to arrange the male guardian's consent to his ward's choice of spouse through a standard scene of revelation in the play, whereas such a resolution would not have been possible in the novel.[22] Henri Giroud could never say to his daughter, as Francoeur does, "Je ratifie le don que tu as fait ... de ton coeur & de ta personne. Aimez vous, aimez la patrie. Que la vertu vous honore & puisse la calomnie vous épargner!" (406) [I confirm the gift you have made ... of your heart and of your self. Love each other, love the motherland. Let virtue honor you and let calumny spare you!]. Francoeur can give his blessing to Victorine and the man of her choice because he is solidly established in the new social order. Such a happy ending, in the case of the next protagonist under consideration, is as impossible as it would be for Henriette. Like Henriette, Honorine will confront an insurmountable obstacle in trying to marry the man she loves, but this obstacle does not come from an oppositional parent.

Published as the last novel in *Trois femmes*, *Honorine d'Userche* is narrated in the first person by the Abbé de la Tour, and it begins, as do the other parts of *Trois femmes*, with a philosophical conversation involving the abbé and a few other characters.[23] However, it is also related, perhaps even more closely, to *Henriette et Richard* at several different levels. The first is chronological. Although *Honorine d'Userche* is part of *Trois femmes*, the action in *Honorine d'Userche* antedates the action in *Trois femmes* because the context of *Honorine d'Userche* is revolutionary France and that of *Trois femmes* is the world of the emigration, specifically Germany, where the protagonist and her parents have sought refuge after losing their possessions.[24] *Honorine d'Userche*, then, is linked more closely to *Henriette et Richard* because both novels make 1788 a significant date. One of Honorine's letters is dated 30 October 1788, and the abbé remarks: "On était pour ainsi dire à la veille de la révolution" (9:204) [We were, so to speak, on the eve of the Revolution]. Similarly, Henriette's first letter to Richard is dated 29 December 1788, as previously mentioned. As in *Henriette et Richard*, the characters in *Honorine d'Userche* are affected by revolutionary events. For example, Honorine manipulates her mother into leaving Paris at one point by inciting in her anxiety about the physical violence in the streets (211).[25] One wonders if she did not have Henriette in mind when she created Honorine: they are both heroines who do not marry the man of their choice and they are both set in the context of revolutionary France. In each novel there is an abbé who guides the young couple. In each novel the young lover moves to be at a distance from the heroine toward the end. The difference between the two novels is the form of the obstacle the heroine encounters. If *Honorine d'Userche* is viewed, as *Henriette et Richard* was in this chapter, from the perspective of the treatment of woman in revolutionary ideology, then these obstacles do not differ so significantly from one another. Indeed, the two novels may be complementary. While Henriette cannot marry Richard unless her father gets the girl of his dreams, Honorine cannot marry the man of her choice because he turns out to be her brother and refuses to commit incest. Applying Lynn Hunt's Freudian interpretation of the Revolution to *Honorine d'Userche* will show the extent to which this novel is thoroughly grounded in the creation of a new social order of men, making the impasse plotted for Honorine complementary to that plotted for Henriette.

In *Honorine d'Userche,* a recently married young noblewoman becomes so wanton that she produces not one but two bastards during her husband's extended absence: first a boy, Florentin, and then a girl, Honorine. The mother disposes of Florentin, immediately sending him away to be raised in total ignorance of his lineage. Honorine, born after the husband's return (and his dismay), will be raised by him: "Il s'attacha à l'enfant autant qu'il se dégoutta de la mere" (180) [He became as attached to the child as he was disgusted by the mother]. It is by accident that the husband buys property in the same area where Florentin lives and by accident that the two young children bond to one another. Soon they are in love, and Charrière's description of Honorine's love, because of the intensity with which she paints it, is unique in her oeuvre (192–93). Honorine herself is a unique character, and in this she differs from the conservative, well-behaved Henriette. Honorine is best described as "une admirable applanisseuse de difficultés" (189) [an admirable smoother-over of difficulties]. [26] She manipulates, arranges, and deceives, adopting whatever stratagem will keep her near Florentin.

The outrageous quality of her character emerges most forcefully when the inevitable discovery of their blood tie is revealed during one of their rendezvous. Florentin, who has just learned the terrible news, approaches Honorine. She sees that he is terribly upset (217), but then responds with "sang froid" to the news and then urges that they flee to some place where they can live together without regard for what she dismisses as "un préjugé" [a belief], telling Florentin that in anticipation of such a disaster she has come wearing men's clothes under her dress (218). Florentin can neither attain her supreme indifference to the concept of incest nor can he disregard his new-found bond to the man who is his real father: "Chere Honorine, soit faiblesse, soit vertu, je me sens moins de résolution, je plains cet homme ... mon pere" [Dear Honorine, whether it be weakness or virtue, I feel less resolute; I pity this man ... my father]. As soon as the blood tie between Florentin and Honorine — or rather, I would suggest, that between Florentin and his father — is revealed, Honorine and Florentin follow different paths. Honorine commits to their sexual relationship, a relationship excluding the father, and Florentin commits to filiation, a filiation exclusive of any sexual relationship with Honorine. The novels ends after Florentin and their father go to Italy, while Honorine and their mother emigrate to Germany under the threat of increasing antiaristocratic violence in France. Honorine decides that

Florentin was killed in a battle, since he has not written to her, and the concluding sentence of *Honorine d'Userche* represents her wandering alone, mourning.

What can we make of a heroine who so hungrily embraces the idea of an incestuous love for her brother and of the brother who rejects her so irrevocably? Hunt has taken Freud's family romance as a key to understanding the link that may be observed in late eighteenth-century France between representations of familial relationships and actual political events. Incest, as a literary theme, reflects the anxiety over the new social order being created after the murder of the father/king; more specifically, it reflects the fear that men and women would cease being different. Hunt makes the point that "in virtually all pre-Sade novels about incest, the lovers are not guilty because they did not know of their family relationship before the deed was committed."[27] Seen in this light, Honorine is more than unique: she is outrageous because she is prepared to commit the deed in full knowledge of the incestuous relationship. On the other hand, Florentin instantly makes secondary his bond with a woman, giving priority to a bond with a man. This character would seem to be acting out the constitution of the public sphere, in which all men are created equal through "liberté, égalité, fraternité" and the exclusion of women.[28] Although Hunt interprets this constitution as taking place through the formation of what Freud terms a "band of *brothers*," I would argue that Florentin's choice of his father over his sister similarly reflects this fraternal bonding. First of all, his choice entails the rejection of woman. Secondly, his relationship with his father, who becomes ill after the revelation scene and requires care rather than obedience, has less the characteristics of the unequal father-son relationship and more those of the equalizing brother-brother relationship.

While in chapter 1 the novels studied showed heroines who subvert the force of stereotyping, the three heroines of the Revolution serve instead to expose the inequity being written into the new bourgeois republic. Henriette and Honorine do not contest any image of woman. They stand instead as a compelling image of the story not told in accounts of the new social order. In this order, Henri will have a foothold, his "justification" having been protected at some cost to his daughter. Florentin will bond with his father, excluding his former love/sister from this bond. In light of the sad fate of these two heroines, the name of the third revolutionary-era heroine, Victorine, resonates with significance.

3

The Last Word on Gendered Discourse: "To Be Continued"

The creation of fictional heroines according to certain conventions is one means by which conformity to socially prescribed roles may be elicited. On a larger scale, fiction is structured by power relationships in a given society. Barbara Herrnstein Smith makes the point that "because literary authority ... tends to be vested differentially along lines of general social and cultural dominance," it follows that "institutionalized literary norms ... tend to have, among other biases, those of gender perspectives."[1] An example of this can be seen in the rigorous exposure of the "maleness" of philosophical discourse that Genevieve Lloyd has undertaken, showing a way for feminists to uncover the effects of discourse and to change the ways in which we think.[2] The focus of this chapter is a comparison of two novels so as to illustrate ways in which the relationship between gender and discourse may be helpfully exposed.[3] In the eighteenth century, the difference between masculine and feminine discourse subtended the distinction made between the objective entries in the *Encyclopédie* and the subjective letters of the popular epistolary novels.[4] This distinction, linking the rational and objective to the masculine and the emotional and subjective to the feminine, marks two of Charrière's novels, *Lettres écrites de Lausanne* (1785/87), an epistolary novel featuring letters by a female character, and *Sir Walter Finch et son fils* (1799/1806), a memoir-novel narrated by a male character in the role of a philosophe.

The former has been the object of a great deal of critical attention — indeed it is Charrière's most famous novel — while the latter has been relatively neglected. Yet, *Lettres écrites de Lausanne* resembles *Sir*

Walter Finch et son fils by virtue of their unusual form: both are two-part novels in which the sequel (of almost the same length) has a different narrator than does the first part. The sequel to *Lettres écrites de Lausanne* is entitled *Caliste, ou Continuation des Lettres écrites de Lausanne; seconde partie*; the sequel to *Sir Walter Finch et son fils* is entitled *Suite des Finch; Sir Walter Finch et son fils William*.[5] One way to account for this form would be to refer to Charrière's reputation for not finishing her novels, and to see in her addition of a sequel with a different narrator a refusal to conclude the first part of the novel. However, reading *Lettres écrites de Lausanne* and *Sir Walter Finch et son fils* with regard to this unusual form reveals that these two novels both question the authority of literary form by combining two parts (the first part and a sequel) in such a way as to deconstruct a given type of gendered discourse. The sequel, then, would stand not as a refusal of closure but as the equivalent of a "to be continued" marker, suggesting that the relationship between the two parts is part of an ongoing process. Because in each of these novels Charrière creates a plot in which gender is thematized, this process must concern gender. Put quite simply, *Lettres écrites de Lausanne* modifies the typically feminine voice of the monophonic epistolary novel, and *Sir Walter Finch et son fils* modifies the supposedly masculine voice of objective philosophic discourse. In so doing, Charrière's readers confront the basis for their expectations as readers, thereby perpetuating the reader/text confrontation inscribed in *Sainte Anne*.

To Bring Out a Woman's Voice — *Lettres écrites de Lausanne*

In a letter dated 27 August 1793, Madame de Staël complained about Charrière's first novel: "Je me suis intéressée vivement aux lettres neufchateloises mais je ne sais rien de plus pénible que votre manière de commencer sans finir, ce sont des amis dont vous nous séparez" (4:162) [I was very interested in *Lettres neuchâteloises*, but I know of nothing more painful than your way of beginning without concluding; these are friends from whom you are separating us]. She goes on to flatter Charrière: "Je ne sais rien que je préferasse au plaisir de lire sans cesse un roman de vous, je crois que cela suspendroit la révolution et que ce monde chimérique deviendroit le mien" (4:163) [I know of nothing that I prefer to the pleasure of continually reading one of your novels; I believe that it would suspend the Revolution and that this fantasy world would become mine]. De Staël's comment represents well the different directions taken in the history of Charrière criticism. Early critics saw in her an interesting lady writing to escape her own tedium; they viewed her novels as trivial. Then, critics who were concerned with recognizing neglected women novelists of the eighteenth century, saw in her someone whose lucidity concerning the feminine condition led her to outline pessimistic sketches that were necessarily unfinished. Most recent feminist critics have tended to see her as an author who sought to contest the social reality of women rather than to create a "monde chimérique." These are critics 'for whom the issue of closure is of paramount importance. Joan DeJean, for example, defines experimentation with closure as a distinguishing feature of novels by women: "Th[e] repeated rejection of fictional and civil closure, coupled with the simultaneous inscription of literary and legal disorder, can be seen as the founding gesture of the tradition of French women's writing."[6] It could be argued that the issue of closure has been Charrière's passport out of French literary history and into feminist criticism. Essays dealing with the dissatisfaction so bluntly expressed by de Staël that may be caused by Charrière's conclusions now tend to focus on her modification of traditional narrative form as a means of inscribing a protest.[7]

While Charrière's *Lettres de Mistriss Henley* has been studied with reference to its lack of closure, the novel that is most often analyzed in these terms is *Lettres écrites de Lausanne*. The two tangentially linked parts of this text feature not only two different narrators but also two vastly different protagonists. In the first part, a mother writes to a female friend about her efforts to marry off her daughter, Cécile. The daughter, being Protestant and lacking an enticing dowry, represents a difficult case. At the end of the novel, the two women leave town, more or less giving up on the young English lord who may or may not have been interested in Cécile. The second part — *Caliste, ou Continuation des Lettres écrites de Lausanne; seconde partie* — consists almost entirely of a letter to this first narrator from William, the mentor of the indecisive English lord. William tells Cécile's mother the story of his own sad life. He loved Caliste, a demimondaine, but he was unwilling or unable to disobey his father's prohibition against marrying a woman of such questionable repute. Although they each married someone else, the novel concludes with William's boundless grief when he learns of her death. Thus Cécile's conclusion seems to leave her in limbo, while that of Caliste features her grandiloquent deathbed scene. At first glance it would seem that Charrière had concluded an inconclusive novel with one that was overly conclusive. Not surprisingly, critics have sought to account for the strangeness of this form, working out different answers to the question of whether the story of Caliste in any way concludes that of Cécile. [8]

In contrast to previous critics, I propose a reading of Charrière's most famous novel that neither compares the first part to the sequel nor splits the novel into two incompatible parts. Few critics have taken into account the three one-page sequels to the sequel. [9] These sequels, identified by the editors of the *Oeuvres complètes* as three fragments of a sequel to the novel (8:617), are important, — even if they are obviously just sketches for where Charrière might take the novel — because they each repeat or duplicate the narrative break that occurs between the first part, with the female narrator's letters to a friend, and the second part, with William's confession. The genre thus created in *Lettres écrites de Lausanne* exploits the capacity of the epistolary novel to take on more narrators and more text: what the first page of *Caliste, ou Continuation des Lettres écrites de Lausanne* lists as "quelques-unes des lettres que les personnes que nous avons fait connoître ont dû s'écrire depuis" (182) [some of the letters that the persons we have made known must have written to each other since then]. [10] The following chart indicates the relationship between all five parts of *Lettres écrites de Lausanne*, giving the titles by which I will refer to them:

Part	Narrator	Addressee	Topic
First	Cécile's mother	a female friend	Cécile to wed?
Continuation	almost exclusively William	Cécile's mother	William's love for Caliste
Sequel I	Cécile's mother	William	William's grief
Sequel II	Edouard's father	William	Edouard
Sequel III	Cécile	her mother	Cécile is married

If these sequels are added to the text, then *Lettres écrites de Lausanne* stands not as a two-part novel beginning with a monophonic epistolary novel, but as a one-part polyphonic epistolary novel. At first glance it would seem that, in adding these sequels, which are disparate but not mutually contradictory, Charrière is doing nothing more than taking advantage of the epistolary form: new characters could be introduced and letters could be added to further complicate the plot without the author's being obliged to rewrite the whole novel. However, the consideration of *Lettres écrites de Lausanne* along with sequels I, II, and III suggests that the representation of woman's voice is being modified in a significant manner. There is an evolution from a preliminary form, the monophonic epistolary novel with a female narrator, to a final form, the polyphonic epistolary novel with both male and female narrators. This is not suppressing woman's voice but rather liberating it from what was an inhibiting literary convention. In the monophonic epistolary novel with a female narrator, woman's voice is modeled on that of the solitary *épistolière*. This figure was derived, in the course of literary history, from what Elizabeth C. Goldsmith calls "the suffering, passionate woman."[11] Such a narrator is perceived as pouring her anguish into the type of love letters that although suitable for publication were not empowering. With regard to a parallel distinction, Landes emphasizes that eighteenth-century women could be letter writers, but they were not, in general, the editors of collected correspondences, "a much more assertive and self-conscious role."[12] The monologic epistolary novel with a female narrator is overdetermined by precisely this limited and limiting type of gendered discourse. The perniciousness of this image is succinctly brought out in Miller's unsparing comparison of the twentieth-century *The Story of O* with the seventeenth-century *The Portuguese Letters*. She asserts: "for me the pornography of female submission is no more than — surely no worse than — the embodiment of sentimental masochism."[13] This conflation of physical and emotional violence against women may serve to assess Charrière's innovation: by structuring *Lettres écrites de Lausanne* along the lines of a novel that begins with, and then abandons, the feminized discourse of the monologic epistolary novel, she liberates woman's voice from a destructive literary convention.

The consequences of such a liberation from the inhibiting feminine voice are prefigured in a famous digression. Writing to her woman friend about what concerns women, the narrator (Cécile's mother) digresses from this subject matter at one point to elaborate an alternative political structure. What begins as a criticism of the nobility in Lausanne is pursued in the language of a fantasy about an ideal noble class: "J'avoue que j'ai ces autres dans la tête plutôt que ne les connois. J'imagine des gens" (141) [I confess that I have these others in my head instead of knowing them. I imagine people]. However, she soon adopts a thoroughly political type of discourse as she elaborates on her idea of a new nobility.[14] She renovates not just class structure but the role of gender by proposing that men would marry into their wife's class, not vice versa. Her private concerns resurface at this point as she imagines Cécile with suitors at her feet: "Tous les jeunes hommes de sa propre classe, qui ne voudroient pas déchoir, & ceux d'une classe inférieure, qui auroient l'ambition de s'élever" [All the young men of her class who would not like to sink in rank and those of an inferior class who would have the ambition to elevate themselves]. Not surprisingly, her female correspondent responds to reading these political ideas by handing the letter over to a man, her husband, so that he is the one who formulates comments and objections to these ideas. Engaging in a debate with him on the matter, Cécile's mother delineates clearly that by entering political discourse, she has crossed gender lines. She sets off his objections in single quotation marks and responds to each one logically until she reaches the one objection to which there is no logical answer: "'Il est bien d'une femme', dites-vous: à la bonne heure, je suis une femme, & j'ai une fille.... j'ai du foible pour mon sexe" [It's definitely by a woman, you say. Indeed, I am a woman and I have a daughter.... I favor my own gender]. She concludes her letter by returning to appropriate female discourse: "Je vous remercie de m'avoir répondu si gravement.... Adieu, mon cousin. Je retourne à votre femme" (147) [I thank you for having answered me so seriously.... Farewell, cousin. I am going back to your wife].

The digression made by the female narrator when she shifts from the feminine, private language of women's concerns to the masculine, public language of political discourse is clearly marked as a transgression of gender lines. However, this does not represent the silencing of the feminine voice. On the contrary, the evidence of this transgression in the political discourse she adopted is vindicated as a woman's presence: "Indeed, I am a woman and I have a daughter." Such a vindication of a female presence parallels what happens with the liberation of woman's voice from the feminized, monophonic epistolary novel, and its integration into the polyphonic epistolary novel. The consideration of

Lettres écrites de Lausanne as an whole, including the continuation and the three sequels, reveals the form of a new woman-to-woman discourse that might give an unconventional voice to woman while respecting the boundaries of a narrowly defined eighteenth-century genre.

It is not just the form of the discourse but the plot that vindicates woman's identity. What is plotted in *Lettres écrites de Lausanne* is maternal love; as we shall see, this plot is foregrounded by the sequels. Instead of a conventional epistolary novel about heterosexual love, we are presented with one about asexual maternal love; the male/female difference is replaced by the female/female identity. This is an important change in perspective because it makes secondary an affective relationship that still today tends to be seen as primary. In the following consideration of the three sequels, we will see how they have the effect of subsuming the relationship between William and Caliste, the subject matter of the Continuation, into the larger context of the relationship between Cécile's mother and Cécile. Treating the three sequels as the conclusion to the novel will make clear the creative aspect of Charrière's text.

Sequel I, the letter from Cécile's mother to William responding to his sad confession about Caliste, begins rather brutally: "Que faites-vous Malheureux homme. Vivez vous?" (239) [What are you doing, unhappy man. Are you alive?] The mother's response to his tale of woe is to reduce Caliste to a point of comparison, displacing Caliste from the unique focal point she occupied in his confession and from the role normally given to the dead female love object. The text of the letter sets in motion a series of substitutions involving Caliste. First she is assimilated to a class of asexual beings when Cécile's mother points out how William might have avoided his grief. [15] Next her status as unique love object for William is undermined when the narrator wonders why the grief he felt over the death of his brother did not preclude his running the risk of having this second love object die. The beginning and end of the letter frame this series of substitutions by making of Caliste nothing more than a point of comparison for Cécile. Cécile's mother begins by comparing his grief to what hers would be if she lost Cecile. She concludes by imagining that even if Caliste were alive, as Cécile is, William would be as unable to protect her from a fatal accident (such as being hit by a rock or slipping on a stone), as Cécile's mother is unable to protect her daughter:

Et moi qui me vantois tout-à l'heure de veiller à la conservation de Cecile &
de mon bonheur je la laissois ... se promener avec les filles de l'aubergiste &
l'on m'a dit hier ... qu'il y avoit quelquefois des serpens dans les prairies.
(240)

[And I, who was bragging just now about watching over Cécile's safety and
my happiness, I was letting her ... take a walk with the innkeeper's daughters
and I was told yesterday ... that there were sometimes snakes in the
meadows.]

To think here of the serpent from Eden seems inappropriate, given the
conservative behavior of Cécile (and of Caliste, who never gives herself
to William). On the other hand, the reference to accidents does bring the
exalted love object down into the less exalted corporeal reality of scraped
knees and nosebleeds.

Making of Caliste a point of comparison for Cécile integrates this
sequel well into the body of the novel as a whole for two reasons. First of
all, we have seen how it makes of Caliste's death a lesson for Cécile's
mother. Similarly, the preceding part (*Caliste, ou Continuation des
Lettres écrites de Lausanne*) began with a death that served as a lesson.
Before William's long epistolary confession, there appears one letter
from Cécile's mother to her female correspondent recounting the death of
an abandoned black servant. Cécile, after insisting on watching over him,
observes him die. Her mother makes of this simple, stark death a lesson
for Cécile after which she will not perceive death in a superstitious or
fearful way (187). Cécile's reaction to the man's death, "C'est donc ainsi
qu'on finit, maman" [So, then, that's how one comes to an end, Mother],
will be echoed in the last letter of *Caliste*. Writing to inform William that
Caliste has finally expired, her husband states, "Ainsi a fini votre
Caliste" (234) [That's how your Caliste came to an end]. It is Caliste's
death that Charrière presents, in Sequel I, as a lesson for Cécile's mother:
"And I, who was bragging just now about watching over Cécile's
safety...." Sequel I is integrated into the even larger context of *Lettres
écrites de Lausanne* through its reduction of Caliste to a point of
comparison for Cécile: the very first letter of the novel begins by making
the daughter of the narrator's correspondent, a young girl who has just
been married off, a point of comparison for Cécile (137). Thus, Sequel I,
despite its relative brevity and its lack of editing, coheres to the
beginnings of both the first and second parts of the novel. More

significantly, the way in which Sequel I is integrated serves to subsume William's confession with its plot about heterosexual love into the narration of Cécile's mother with its plot about maternal love.[16]

That the structure of this novel is formulated on making maternal discourse dominant would seem to be confirmed by Sequel II. Just as we went from Cécile's mother to a male narrator in shifting from the first to the second part, in shifting from Sequel I to Sequel II we go from Cécile's mother to Edouard's father. Once again, this should not be read as a silencing of the female voice. The concern that Edouard's father expresses about his son is a masculine equivalent of the concern of Cécile's mother. Each worries about molding the child into what society requires. Cécile must enter society ("le monde") if she is to be seen by a potential spouse.[17] But as a young woman, she must respect the limits imposed on her by society. The description that Edouard's father makes of his son's behavior in society sounds like a male version of this prob-lem and thus highlights the gendered difference between what each child faces. As a young man, Edouard must not abuse his male prerogative to exceed the limits imposed on him by society.[18] Significantly, each parent sees in a familial relationship a possible solution to the problem. Cécile's mother, a pawn in a patrilinear society, looks to her grandfather. She imagines that, had he gone to mass, she would have had a better chance of marrying off her daughter: "Je ne sais s'il s'en trouveroit aussi bien dans l'autre monde; mais moi, il me semble que je m'en trouverois mieux dans celui-ci" (138) [I don't know if this way he would have been better off in the next world but as for me, I believe that I would be better off in this one]. In contrast, Edouard's father looks to future progeny for a solution to his feeling that perhaps Edouard does not have the material necessary to be a scion in due and proper form. His father's regret over three infants who did not survive is intensified by the realization that if Edouard is not turning out as he should by now, he is a lost cause. However, unlike Cécile's mother, he does not have to wish that the past were changed, for his wife is expecting (243). The difference in the familial relationship to which Cécile's mother and Edouard's father look reflects the ordering of ancien régime society: women were the conduits for transmitting patrilinear descent.

In considering the novel as a whole, Sequel II fits in by repeating, in its relation to Sequel I, the female/male shift in narrator, and by transposing a mother's concern for her daughter with a father's concern for his son. We also see the Cécile/Caliste shift repeated. The conclusion of the letter from Edouard's father is structured by an ellipsis representing the space in which Cécile's place is taken by Caliste. Wishing that Edouard had had the incentive to marry Cécile, his father imagines taking care of her and enjoying her company but then breaks off, a break that is punctuated by an ellipsis. Following the ellipsis, he states he has learned of the death of that beautiful woman, without specifying Caliste's name. In his letter, then, he goes from discussing one woman, Cécile, to referring briefly to a different one, Caliste, thereby repeating the Cécile/Caliste shift in the plot.

The maternal discourse that was echoed by the paternal discourse in Sequel II will be concluded in Sequel III when the most significant affective and discursive relationship in the novel, that between Cécile and her mother, is disrupted. This final letter, in which we will learn that the mother/daughter bond has been split by marriage, concludes *Lettres écrites de Lausanne* in a definitive manner. [19] Even more remarkable, however, is that Cécile, so long an object of her mother's discourse, becomes a narrator in her own right. Suite III consists of her only letter, and it stages her acquiring an independent voice through separation from her mother. This sequel provides half an answer to the question concerning a spouse for Cécile. In answer to the specific question, Will she marry Edouard? we learn that she did not; but there is no answer to the larger question, Whom will she marry? We are given only a reference to an unidentified husband who is devoted to Cécile's mother (247). The wedding and the details of the marriage, then, are suppressed in a letter whose function appears at first to be to perpetuate the seamless mother/daughter bond. This would be consistent with the domination of the maternal discourse that we have observed so far. However, this concluding letter actually puts an end to this domination and, by so doing, puts an end to the novel.

Suite III is the shortest one (only half a page long). It consists largely of the expression of Cécile's love for her mother. In fact, the letter begins with the pronoun "nous" (we), which, in light of her status as a married woman one might expect to refer to Cécile and her husband. Because it is qualified by "tous" (all), however, it refers to Cécile and her mother with the addition of the new husband: "Nous avons tous fait ce que nous devions chere Maman il ne faut donc pas s'attrister ni se plaindre mais cette separation est bien cruelle" (247) [We have all done what we should, dear mother, so we must not feel sad or complain, but this separation is very cruel]. This threesome is not a unit that can survive, and the letter will actually sever Cécile from her mother. Having pointed out that letters can never substitute for physical presence, which implies that the mother/daughter bond is weakened by the act of writing, Cécile evokes the only other letter (besides the one that she is writing) that she ever wrote to her mother. This letter is not featured in *Lettres écrites de Lausanne,* so Cécile's reference to the letter has two simultaneous effects. On the one hand, Cécile's present letter makes the previous letter present by referring to it. On the other hand, Cécile's present letter makes the previous letter absent by making known its absence. In fact, this simultaneous making present/making absent is what she does with her mother in this letter.

> Voici la seconde lettre que je vous écrive de ma vie. Vous souvient-il de la premiere? Si votre voyage est allé aussi bien que je l'espere vous passerez demain devant le couvent où je l'ecrivis. C'etoit le lendemain du jour où je declarai à [Edouard] que je ne voulois plus de lui. J'etois encore bien emue en vous ecrivant.

> [Here is the second letter that I have ever written to you. Do you remember the first? If your trip has gone as well as I hope, you will pass tomorrow in front of the convent where I wrote it. It was the day after I declared to Edouard that I no longer wanted to have anything to do with him. I was still deeply affected while writing to you.]

The link here between mother and daughter is the location that they share in common, a convent, and this location serves to define them as now separate. A letter can never substitute for physical presence, making the convent both the space from which Cécile wrote her first letter to her mother and the space from which an absence between mother and daughter was instituted.[20] Although this space is evoked as a point in common (*"you* will pass tomorrow in front of the convent where *I* wrote it"), it can only distance mother and daughter, since now "where you are" is "where I am not," as proven by the letter that Cécile is writing. While the presence of the mother in the heretofore seamless mother/daughter bond is explicitly affirmed in this letter, the form of this affirmation — the convent as a point in common — erases this presence. Just as the reference to the first letter Cécile ever wrote to her mother made this letter present but did so by designating its absence from the novel, so in this last letter to her mother Cécile makes her present and in so doing concretizes her absence. This letter necessarily concludes the novel because the most important affective relationship (the mother/daughter bond) and the dominant discursive relationship (maternal discourse with Cécile as object) have been brought to an end.[21]

If all parts of this novel are considered as a whole, then we might read it as the story of making heard a woman's voice. The sequels to *Lettres écrites de Lausanne* suggest that Charrière manipulated the inherent capacity of the epistolary form to take on new narrators and new text so as to show the woman's voice that is being created in this manner and to have this voice subsume all the others. Once woman's voice has been heard and has been given precedence, the novel ends. By charting the integration of the monophonic epistolary form into the polyphonic, Charrière effects the freeing of woman's voice from what is a gendered form confining her voice to a stereotypical function, a gesture of considerable importance. Consider the conclusion reached by Elizabeth Berg in her comparison of two other literary texts, *Sonnets for Helene* and the *Portuguese Letters*:

> In refusing the unitary, coherent determination of positions ... one may make possible a relationship between writer and reader (or between text and reader) based on congruences, intersections, encounters. Sexual identity ... then becomes a temporary configuration, structuring a particular relationship. It is a partial identity.[22]

In Charrière's novel, what seems to be a refusal of coherence — namely, the proliferation of tangentially related sequels with different narrators — represents precisely this refusal to confine her woman narrator to a socially defined sexual role. Resituating the female narrator in the course of *Lettres écrites de Lausanne*, gives a new meaning to what was, in eighteenth-century literature, an overdetermined term: woman.

Charrière did more than exploit the capacity of the epistolary novel to take on "some of the letters that the persons we have made known must have written to each other since then." With *Lettres écrites de Lausanne,* this capacity makes possible what it was so difficult for the eighteenth-century novel to do: give a voice to woman's subjectivity. Her text is all the more striking if we consider that sequel adding was a capacity that could serve to disappropriate the author's voice. For example, the sequels that other authors provided for Graffigny's *Lettres d'une péruvienne* all perverted the original. Dismayed at the thought that a woman could choose to remain independent and unmarried, they all used the original elements provided by Graffigny to marry off the Peruvian woman and thus ensure proper closure.[23] In contrast, Charrière used the sequel-adding capacity of the epistolary novel to appropriate a woman's voice, with appropriate being understood in its most basic sense: "to assign as private property or possession to; *to set apart for a special purpose*" (*Oxford English Dictionary*; emphasis added). Her structuring of this novel would seem to answer the wish expressed by Hélène Cixous that the female author "get out of the booby-trapped silence!" Cixous insists that "it is in writing, from woman and toward woman, and in accepting the challenge of the discourse controlled by the phallus, that woman will affirm woman somewhere other than in silence."[24] The convention of the suffering letter writer pouring her raw emotions into a letter is precisely the straitjacket from which Charrière's narrator escapes.

That Charrière was indeed innovating, and not deviating from accepted novelistic form, may be confirmed by a consideration of a later novel, *Sir Walter Finch et son fils*. The form of this novel is similar to *Lettres écrites de Lausanne* in that it consists of two parts of almost equal length with two different narrators. However, the form of *Sir Walter Finch et son fils* also differs from the earlier novel in that it does not have any equivalent for the additional sequels. With this next novel under consideration, we will see another instance of the way in which Charrière used form to work on the gendering of a literary text. The goal in this case is to disempower the voice of male objectivity rather than to make heard that of female subjectivity.

To Undermine a Masculine Voice — *Sir Walter Finch et son fils*

As in *Lettres écrites de Lausanne,* the addition of a sequel to *Sir Walter Finch et son fils* creates a shift in narrator and plot. Although the gender of the narrator does not change, the addition of the sequel has repercussions, just as it did in the earlier novel. In *Sir Walter Finch et son fils,* the objective voice of reason is set up and then undermined so that the novel foregrounds the maleness of the voice of reason, a voice which, in the eighteenth century, was "the dominant medium for display of encyclopedic knowledge in Enlightenment fictions."[25] This gesture puts into question the association between maleness and reason.

While in *Lettres écrites de Lausanne* a mother's concern for her daughter was presented in epistolary form, in *Sir Walter Finch et son fils* a father's concern for his son is presented, but in the form of a journal written before the birth of this son. Sir Walter intends the narrative for William so that he may know about himself from the earliest moments of his existence. The entries span nineteen years and conclude when Sir Walter, having decided to travel to America to seek out his illegitimate daughter, stops writing and gives the journal to his son. The content of the journal largely concerns William's education, but there is an important subtext concerning women, a subtext that appears both in the form of conversations about the nature of women and in the form of Sir Walter's love life (or rather, lack thereof).

Before considering the sequel, Charrière's use of the form of a journal novel must be considered. This genre evolved from the memoir-novel of the early eighteenth century. The form of the memoir-novel had served to legitimate the novel by creating the illusion that it was history, not fiction, that was being presented. The journal form (which attained its fullest development only much later) is inherently different because of the temporal aspects. As Philip Stewart explains, the journal novel "is a natural extension of the memoir form, increasing the narrator's contingency by placing him in the middle of events of still uncertain outcome."[26] It is important to point out that in *Sir Walter Finch et son fils*, however, this contingency is subordinated to another feature. As a character, this narrator is defined as father, observer, and philosophe (all male roles). Instead of what we expect from a narrator who is a journal writer, Sir Walter has more of the qualities of a philosophe, even of a *"musty philosopher"* (9:529), as one character calls him. Janet Whatley classifies him as "Charrière's educational experimentalist."[27] In effect, William's childhood is an occasion for Sir Walter to engage in the child-raising debate, as the different roles that he embodies represent a convergence of the issues brought out in the late eighteenth-century debate over Rousseau's *Emile.*[28]

En théorie du moins, [les gens sublimes et à systèmes d'éducation] ... semblent vouloir que la génération présente ne vive que pour la génération future. Je ne vois nulle justice à ce sacrifice qu'on prétend exiger. (528)

[In theory at least, people given to ratiocination and to inventing education systems ... seem to wish that the present generation should live only for the future generation. I see no justice in this sacrifice that is demanded.] [29]

In addition, the way in which Sir Walter's journal is set up places more focus on the narrator's authority concerning what is recorded than on his subjectivity. Despite any personal impressions the father mentions, his purpose is to be an objective observer of the child: "Vous êtes sevré; vous vous portez très-bien.... Vous êtes un très-bel enfant. Vous marchez, mais ne parlez pas encore" (529) [You are weaned; you are very healthy.... You are a handsome child. You walk but do not speak yet]. When the father does make note of his own feelings, it is in the service of recording the child's environment. A telling example of the secondary status accorded to his feelings is evident in the treatment of his long-lasting obsession with a beautiful but unknown woman: "l'inconnue" [the unknown woman]. Her haunting memory would seem to concern primarily the issue of whether or not Sir Walter will ever fall in love, and yet it is presented as the factor that precludes his son from acquiring a stepmother (525).

And what of the narrative that succeeds this philosophic discourse, completing the novel as a whole? *Suite des Finch; Sir Walter Finch et son fils William* is a journal that the son begins writing after reading that of his father. In it, William describes to his father the life he is leading on his own. This second journal ends when William records that he and Tom, a boy with whom he was raised, have decided to return to "nos demeures de petits garçons" [our homes as little boys] in the Finchs' London residence (9:606). While the first part had chronicled William's coming to manhood, the second part reads strangely like his return to childhood. Although there is no theoretical discussion of the nature of woman in this second part, William's experiences with the opposite sex are, like those of his father, defined by not getting the girl.

If we examine the form of the novel, the response by the son to the first part (Sir Walter's journal) subtly alters it, integrating the journal into a dialogic form. This new dialogic aspect of the text is represented in the possibility the son expresses of mailing parts of his journal to his father, as if the journal comprised letters. [30] In addition, the second part features a significant number of letters that William transcribes into his journal, thereby perpetuating the impression that this is more of a letter than a monologic journal. *Sir Walter Finch et son fils* becomes a hybrid genre, combining elements of the journal form with elements of the epistolary form. In this second part, the narrator, no longer an object to be observed but an intuitive subject, has as purpose to respond to an interlocutor:

> En me parlant du passé comme du présent vous m'avés livré votre vie ... vous avés fait de votre expérience la mienne. Je vais en quelque sorte vous imiter. Je vous rendrai compte des impressions que je reçois. Vous savés ce que vous avés fait pour moi. Vous saurés quel parti, quel profit, j'en tire. (567–68)

> [By speaking to me of the past as of the present, you have given me your life ... you have made your experience mine. I will in a way imitate you. I will keep track for you of what makes an impression on me. You know what you have done for me. You will know what my take is on it, what profit I draw from it.]

The son narrates his reactions to reading his father's journal, "mon trésor" (568) [my treasure]. In contrast to his father, William gives precedence to his impressions instead of his observations. Young William is clearly more of a journal writer than a *philosophe*. The way in which each narrator describes his meeting with a desired woman proves this.

As previously mentioned, Sir Walter was obsessed with a beautiful, unknown woman. He saw her only once out on the road. He told his friend, Lord Frederic, about her, and she was often the topic of their conversations. Their fantasies about this woman came to an abrupt end at a moment when Lord Frederic was away on a voyage. Sir Walter makes a note of this development in his journal, writing bluntly, "Je viens d'apprendre une chose bien singulière. L'inconnue étoit lady Mary **, et lord Frederic ... l'a épousée" (529) [I have just learned a most peculiar fact. The unknown woman was Lady Mary **, and Lord Frederic ... married her]. Years later, Sir Walter is invited to come and visit them. The entry describing the visit is a short one: "Il ne serviroit de rien, mon cher William, de vous détailler comment j'ai passé mon tems ... chez lord Frederic" (538) [It would be useless, my dear William, to describe to you how I spent my time ... at Lord Frederic's]. Suppressing any reference to his reaction upon seeing the long-lost woman of his dreams, he makes of the journal entry a lesson in pedagogy by describing an interaction between lord Frederic and his daughter. Thus Sir Walter's meeting with the desired woman ends up being narrated in such a way as to lead to a pedantic conclusion. "Les instructions morales sont malheureusement trop pleines de contradictions et de confusion" [Moral dictates are unfortunately too full of contradictions and confusion].

Like his father, William falls for a woman who is overdetermined by fantasy. Miss Melvil is distantly related to William through an inheritance he received. Knowing where she lives, he thinks about her.[31] The focus in the description of his meeting with the desired woman is on William's embarrassment. Fearful and stuttering, he invites his reader (his father) to share these feelings: "Imaginez ma surprise quand j'ai vu Miss Melvil.... Il m'a fallu du tems pour prendre une contenance" (570) [Imagine my surprise when I saw Miss Melvil.... It took me a while to compose myself]. The conversation involving him, Miss Melvil, and her mother, as transcribed in his journal entry, sets up a sharp contrast with the lesson in pedagogy that was narrated by his father. Blushing like a beet, he apologizes to the mother: "Vous me faites appercevoir Madame que je suis un impertinent" [You make me realize, ma'am, that I am impertinent]. The marked difference in the descriptions made by each narrator of the meeting with a desired woman shows clearly how the voice in the first part is characterized by philosophical objectivity, whereas that in the second part is characterized by individual subjectivity.

The contrast between the two narrative voices seems to set them up to represent comparative terms: relative to his son's narration, that of Sir Walter is more objective; relative to his father's narration, that of William is more subjective. The form of the novel at this point would tend to refute any absolute quality attributed to the voice of the philosophe since its objectivity is only relative to another voice, not founded on any unmediated relationship to truth. Furthermore, the way in which the authority of the male voice is undermined will be intensified by the relationship that is set up between the two texts at the level of plot. This relationship is manifested in the chronology and family history plotted throughout the son's journal.

From the beginning, William's future is expressed in terms of his father's past. William begins by recording his plans to journey to Cambridge, the location where Sir Walter first saw "the unknown woman" along the roadside.[32] Not only does the son deliberately try to follow backwards his father's path, but he seems fated to relive his father's experience. Just as Sir Walter lost the unknown woman to another man, so William will lose Miss Melvil first to a friend who almost marries her and then to a man who does marry her (591). In fact, the disappearance of a woman is a point around which the two narratives, that of the father and that of the son, cohere. At the conclusion of the first part, Sir Walter had just interviewed a young woman, Miss Brown, who seemed to be a good prospect for William. However, as a result of the interview, both Miss Brown and Sir Walter decide that the marriage is out of the question. Sir Walter's journal then quickly concludes, and that of his son begins. In his very first entry, William deals the final blow to Miss Brown, writing simply that she has been forgotten (567). The shift from the father's journal to that of the son is made around the axis of a woman who is denied entry into their masculine family structure.

Not only does the son seem to repeat or relive his father's life, but the father-son bond is presented as overdetermined. After her death, William's mother is so thoroughly obliterated from the context of the father-son bond that Sir Walter sometimes thinks that he is a bachelor [garçon] rather than a widower (530). This bond is duplicated in other forms of familial relationships. Father and son are also brothers to each other because William was suckled by his father's "soeur de lait" (520).[33] In addition, the father-son bond is inverted when William becomes like a father to Sir Walter, teaching him how to care for an older parent. As Sir Walter dutifully notes, "J'apprends de mon enfant à soigner ma vieille parente" (546) [I am learning from my child how to care for my old relative]. No doubt the most striking illustration of the priority given to the father-son bond is evident in the list that Sir Walter imagines when he reflects upon the type of woman that he would want his son to marry. After each type of woman that he considers, he writes "no" until he arrives at the last possibility: "Voudrois-je d'une bru comme ... votre mère? Hélas! peut-être" (557) [Would I wish for a daughter-in-law like ... your mother? Alas — perhaps]. For his part, William seems similarly limited to male familial relationships. Thus, a young boy with whom he was raised expresses his love for William in these terms: "Vous êtes vous.... le nourrisson de ma mere, mon frere de lait, mon camarade d'enfance, mon ami & mon protecteur dans ma jeunesse" (585) [You are you ... the suckling of my mother, my "frère de lait," my childhood friend, my friend and my protector in my youth].[34]

It is difficult to imagine that young William could be headed for marriage and fatherhood. Can the boy that Sir Walter raised ever become a man? To the contrary, the development of William's life seems to progress backwards in time to his "little boys' room." The impact of William's life story as it is recorded in *Suite des Finch; Sir Walter Finch et son fils William*, a life story during the course of which the son never marries or becomes a father, is to erase the primacy of the father's text. There would be no difference between the idea that the father engendered the son by making him be what he is (a reproduction of his father), or that the son recreated the father by reliving the life his own father lived. Instead of a structure that would represent patrilinear descent, we have a circular structure. The connection between these two parts of *Sir Walter Finch et son fils* provides the key to the significance of the novel's structure. At the level of plot, the life of Sir Walter leads to the life of his son, which repeats the life of Sir Walter. At the level of narration, the sequel (William's journal responding to his father's) should provide some type of verification of what his father-pedagogue-philosophe wrote in the first part. Because this verification is lacking, the validity of the voice in the first part cannot be confirmed. We can know only its excessive maleness. The structure given to the male voice in this novel dismantles the very basis of patriarchy: the authority passed from father to son.

In considering *Sir Walter Finch et son fils* and its sequel, we find that the narrative effects an echo, as the father's narrative is answered by the son's, and that this second narrative is then plotted as a repetition. Weighing equally the father's narrative and that of the son makes it impossible to privilege the philosophical discourse over the subjective discourse. If we focus on the formal aspect of this ending, it seems that Charrière was questioning the notion of the objective male voice by setting it up as one of two poles — the objective and the subjective — and by saturating the narrative with maleness. The voice of the father-pedagogue-philosophe is thereby presented simultaneously as more (but not absolutely) objective and as confined to a male perspective. Given that "the existence of more than one sex problematizes the universality of any human subject of knowledge," Barbara Johnson has proposed that "to retain the plurality of forces and desires within a structure that would displace the One-ness of individual mastery could perhaps be labeled a feminization of authority."[35] If so, then the unusual structure in *Sir Walter Finch et son fils* embodies precisely such a feminization — a gesture that is all the more striking, considering the novel's excessive masculinity, which progresses until the exclusive universe of the little boys' room has been attained.

The exploitation of sequels in Charrière's fiction, her reiterated "to be continued," steers readers clear of delusions about gendered discourse. In contrast to the somewhat more conventional texts considered in chapter 1, these two represent a more subtle undertaking: hence the complexity of their structure. They are both demanding in the way that the confrontation with the reader is in *Sainte Anne*. In this instance, we are not asked to decide what is *vraisemblable* but rather whose voice it is.

4

Interpreting Woman's Difference:
Varieties of Pregnancies

One of the most urgent and divisive issues in feminism today concerns the way in which the physical differences between men and women are either emphasized or disregarded. For example, this issue surfaces in literary criticism whenever the notion of "écriture féminine" is invoked. Thus, while an author such as Hélène Cixous celebrates the particularity of woman's writing, specifying "woman is body more than man is.... More body hence more writing," another author, Joyce Carol Oates, asserts that "the serious artistic voice is one of individual *style*, and it is sexless." [1] The issue of woman's difference also surfaces in law, in the form of two different doctrines. [2] As legal scholar Catherine MacKinnon explains, by the terms of one doctrine, that of gender neutrality, women must be treated as if they are the same as men, as if the anatomical differences are irrelevant. However, the opposite principle underlies the doctrine of special protection, according to which women must be treated so as to take into account their physical differences from men. [3] Whether we discuss literary criticism or legal doctrine, woman's difference may not be thought of as a banner around which feminists rally but as a red flag that provokes them to form factions.

In late eighteenth-century France, theorizing woman's difference was no less complex. The issues being debated then paralleled those that inform discussions of feminism today: is woman to be considered the same as man, regardless of her physical differences from him, or is she to be considered as determined by her physical specificity, regardless of her entitlement to political equality? Advocates of women's equality in prerevolutionary France discovered that the arguments proving the

81

equality of all men were both tantalizing and dangerous. These arguments proved to be inapplicable and even detrimental to their cause, as Landes has shown in her analysis of women and the Revolution. Even more importantly, the increasing force of Rousseau's model of woman tended to invalidate the basis for claiming that woman should resemble man in any degree. In his *Emile,* he delineated the difference between men and women that would soon form the basis of a moral imperative judging woman's worth by her domesticity.

> The strictness of the relative duties of the two sexes is not and cannot be the same. When woman complains on this score about unjust man-made inequality, she is wrong. This inequality is not a human institution — or, at least, it is the work not of prejudice but of reason. It is up to the sex that nature has charged with the bearing of children to be responsible for them to the other sex. [4]

The force of this new domesticity, which served in part as retribution for the visibility and power of ancien régime noblewomen, was insidious. [5] Elisabeth Badinter, for example, has argued that the very concept of maternal love is a creation of late eighteenth- and early nineteenth-century society. She finds that the status assigned to maternal love reflected a political agenda, an agenda directed at tying women to the babies they bore and to their homes so as to exclude them from political life. [6] The controversy about woman's difference such as it was articulated two hundred years ago seems strangely familiar in light of the dilemmas feminists confront today. In this chapter, I discuss the significance to us of Charrière's insights concerning woman's difference. [7] Her insights offer us a way to reconcile gender neutrality with the reality of physical difference, a way to put into reverse the oppression that persists today. As MacKinnon puts it, "Inequality comes first; difference comes after." [8]

On Sexual Difference

Generally speaking, there is a division in Charrière's oeuvre between, on the one hand, her novels, in which she presents a perspicacious analysis of the narrow limits within which society confines women, and, on the other hand, her political works, in which she does not address women's issues in any way whatsoever. The single exception to this division in her oeuvre is constituted by a succinct statement about the insignificance of the difference between men and women; this statement appears in both her novel *Trois femmes* (Three women, 1798) (9:41–168), and her political satire "Lettre d'un Anglois à un député de l'Assemblée nationale de France," mentioned in chapter 2. In both the novel and the satire, she sets up a character who advocates sexual equality by dismissing the importance of physical difference. In "Lettre d'un Anglois," the fictional Englishman admits he is in favor of the equality that would be established if women did have political rights, articulating his opinion in the following terms: Concerning the "facultés de l'homme naissant et tel qu'il sort du ventre de sa mere" [faculties of man at birth and such as he emerges from the womb of his mother], he claims:

> On ne peut disputer quelles ne soient très semblables chez l'un et l'autre sexe et que *les differences qu'on aperçoit* n'entrainent pas l'inégalité qu'on n'aperçoit point. (10:317; emphasis added)

> [One cannot contest that they are very similar in one and the other sex and that *the differences one perceives* do not entail the inequality that one does not perceive.]

In making the original physical similarity between male and female infants the basis for possible political equality, Charrière's Englishman makes sexual difference of secondary importance. But what of a physical phenomenon, such as the risk of becoming pregnant after a rape or of dying in childbirth, that makes woman's sexual difference from man a matter of life or death? Woman's capacity for childbearing constitutes what MacKinnon calls a "doctrinal embarrassment" to those who equate gender neutrality with political equality.[9] It is frustrating that in "Lettre d'un Anglois" this statement from so astute a thinker as Charrière is no more important than a throwaway sentence in a political satire. The narrator does not develop it any further, moving on instead to the topic of equality between upper and lower classes, thereby effacing the question of women's equality.

Less than ten years later, Charrière returned to the issue raised in her Englishman's letter, but this time she did so in a work that is much longer and not satirical. This novel, *Trois femmes*, has the further advantage of being a feminocentric novel. Here, the commentary on sexual difference is presented by a woman. A widow of independent means, Constance, undertakes an experiment in gender. She assumes responsibility for a pair of twins, one male and one female, whose mother died in childbirth. Constance sends them to a wet nurse and arranges to pay double the going rate as long as the boy is called Charlotte, the girl Charles, and they are dressed exactly alike. The wet nurse and her husband are peasants whose roles are divided strictly along gender lines. Constance aims to learn whether the boy will resemble the man and the girl the woman. (The results of the experiment are not presented in the novel.)

Constance designed this experiment in the hope of putting an end to the myth of what she terms "les facultés distinctives des deux sexes" (114) [the distinctive faculties of the two sexes]. She inveighs against this myth at length. Pointing out that everyone knows a woman who reasons better than men or a man who is more delicate than women, and sounding like a more assertive version of Charrière's Englishman, she continues:

> Cela devoit suffire, et il devoit être prouvé pour chacun, qu'il n'y avoit rien dans la qualité d'homme et de femme qui déterminât quoique ce soit relativement à nos facultés intellectuelles. Mais à un argument sans réplique, on ne laisse pas d'avoir mille choses à répliquer, et à la fin, pour argument dernier, on en vient à vous dire que cette différence (prétendue) entre le caractere de l'homme et de la femme est un bienfait de la nature. (115)

> [That should suffice and it should be held as proven for everybody that there was nothing in the quality of man and of woman that determined anything whatsoever relative to our intellectual faculties. But to an irrefutable argument people offer a thousand refutations, and in the end, as a final argument, people come around to telling you that this (supposed) difference between the character of man and of woman is a gift from nature.]

Unlike "Lettre d'un Anglois," which provided no elaboration on the statement concerning the lack of significant difference between men and women, *Trois femmes* does provide such elaboration because in this novel and its sequels Charrière explores the implications of one highly charged manifestation of woman's difference: pregnancy. By comparing *Trois femmes* to the other novels in which she represents the phenomenon of pregnancy, it is possible to infer a perspective on sexual difference. I will use this comparison to evaluate the type of gender neutrality that both the fictional Englishman and Constance seem to advocate. Although it would be inappropriate to present Charrière as any kind of active protofeminist, her insights, as they are presented in her fiction, offer us a means to theorize woman's difference while avoiding either a hazardous emphasis on essentialism or an impractical disregard for biology.

The literary representation of pregnancy may be approached from a variety of angles. Margaret Homans, for example, traces the different resonances of "bearing the word" in nineteenth-century English novels. [10] Following a different lead, Susan Stanford Friedman uses reader response to assess the range of effects that may result from using childbirth as a metaphor for producing a literary text. [11] Because my purpose is to illustrate a way of theorizing woman's natural difference according to the terms presented in Charrière's fiction, I will concentrate on the means used to ascribe significance to the pregnant body. The women featured in Charrière's novels were created in a culture where the perspective on woman's body was undergoing a transition of the greatest magnitude, namely the transition from the belief in a one-sex model to the belief in a two-sex model. Thomas Laqueur has charted the epistemological development through which woman's body, once believed to be an inferior form of man's, came to be viewed as that of a creature completely different from him. "Structures that had been thought common to man and woman — the skeleton and the nervous system — were differentiated so as to correspond to the cultural male and female." [12] Changes in the perception of women, not the appearance of any abstract physical reality, had led doctors to these supposedly scientific conclusions. For the purposes of the present discussion, I focus on the "cultural female" as a construct of the fictional text. In the three novels under consideration, comparing the means by which the difference of woman's body is revealed through the representation of pregnancy will illustrate once again how literary conventions are implicated in the oppression of women.

In addition to *Trois femmes*, there are two other novels in which Charrière describes the pregnancy of a character: *Lettres de Mistriss Henley* (1784) and *Lettres neuchâteloises* (1784). Each is narrated in a different form and, as we shall see, the genre of the novel is as pertinent as the character who becomes pregnant. The fate of this woman varies so much among these three novels that it leads to an apparent paradox, for the worst fate befalls the one woman who is married and legitimately pregnant. The best fate, plotted in *Trois femmes*, is reserved for a lady's maid, a young girl who in no way exemplifies the eighteenth-century notion of female virtue. Although Charrière was hardly a slave to convention, it should not be inferred from this that she was advocating free sex instead of married life. Instead, these texts portray a spectrum revealing the range of meanings, from negative to positive, that may be ascribed to woman's physical difference. Each meaning entails specific consequences for the lived experience of a woman, and these consequences are what determine the variety of fates plotted for the women in the three novels. Isolating the literary means by which woman's physical difference is revealed entails beginning with the disclosure of pregnancy made in each novel. Because the source of this disclosure can only be the expectant mother, such a reading assigns priority to woman's body and to her control over it. Next, identifying the role of the father relative to the pregnancy will further refine the way in which woman is being represented. The most logical consequence of pregnancy — childbirth and then child raising — is plotted in only one of the three novels: *Trois femmes*. To conclude, then, I outline the factors Charrière integrates into her description of this consequence in order to show how she theorizes about woman's difference in a thoroughly real and practical manner.

The Disclosure of Pregnancy

Two assessments by scholars concerning pregnancy in the eighteenth-century novel point to Charrière's originality. According to Pierre Fauchery, the pregnancy of the protagonist intensifies the drama of the eighteenth-century feminocentric novel because, given the reality of female mortality during childbirth, it put her life in danger.[13] In the fiction of Charrière, however, her description of a character's pregnancy is not directed at eliciting any dramatic effects, in part because she eschews dramatic effects as such.[14] More pertinently, as we shall see, pregnancy in her novels contributes to a reflection on sexual difference and the problem of woman's inequality.

Within the more specific context of novels by women, Isabelle Brouard-Arens has shown that late-eighteenth-century fiction by women authors is notable for the presence of previously unmentionable physical phenomena associated with pregnancy. The decision made by women to include details about labor and breastfeeding in their novels constituted an effort to destigmatize what were otherwise considered improper details of woman's physicality.[15] The thesis developed by Brouard-Arens tends to organize the novels she reads around the idea of women glorifying their own role in the production of heirs or citizens. Brouard-Arens assimilates Charrière (who never had a child) into this category, although she only considers novels other than *Trois femmes*. This omission leads to an overgeneralization, since it is in *Trois femmes* that the event and consequences of pregnancy dominate the plot. Indeed, in this novel, pregnancy, far from glorifying the role that late-eighteenth-century society assigned to woman, manifests instead the meaning of woman's physical difference from man in an unsentimental light.

The three novels under consideration here fall into a logical progression according to the way the pregnancy is disclosed. Placing priority on the woman's experience, we will begin with the most intimate disclosure. This is in *Lettres de Mistriss Henley,* where the pregnant woman writes of her pregnancy in a letter to a woman friend. Later, in *Lettres neuchâteloises*, a woman will speak, on behalf of a young girl, to a man in order to communicate the information that this girl is with child. This communication takes place during the course of a semiprivate conversation; the conversation involves only three people but it occurs in a crowd at a public gathering. Concerning the most striking disclosure — the one appearing in *Trois femmes* — it can only be said that in this case the news of her condition literally escapes the woman, grabbing the attention of those who are with her. The pregnant woman in no way controls this last disclosure, so I consider it to be the least private, although the circumstances surrounding it are by no means extremely public.

With *Lettres de Mistriss Henley,* Charrière responds to Samuel Constant's *Le Mari sentimental* (1784), a monophonic epistolary novel in which he presents the letters of Mr. Bompré to his male friend. The letters chronicle the descent into suicide of this kindly man after his marriage to a harpy.[16] In her work, also a monophonic epistolary novel, Charrière presents the perspective of a woman married to a man who is the very soul of reason. Unfortunately, this is a cast iron soul, and Mrs. Henley's efforts to please him meet with either his stoic indifference or his reasoned disapproval.[17] Her letters, addressed to a woman friend, degenerate from a discussion of what she had hoped for when she married to the description of a state of catatonic resignation:

> An old lime tree screens a rather charming view from one of my windows.... The best I can do, in this verdant season, is to watch the leaves appear.... I don't understand any of it.... I lose myself in this vast whole that is so wonderful.... I watch, and hours pass during which I have not thought even once about myself or my childish sufferings (35–36).[18]

Just as the suicide of the male protagonist in *Le Mari sentimental* is painted as masculine (through the image of the gun he will use hanging next to his father's portrait), so Mrs. Henley's suicide is painted as feminine (through her rejection of this option precisely on the grounds that she is a woman and, furthermore, pregnant). However, Charrière concludes the novel with the suggestion that her protagonist will die: "In a year, in two years, you will learn, I trust, that I am reasonable and contented, or that I am no more" (43). Commenting on the two options presented here in the light of the eighteenth-century discourse on happiness, Marie-Paule Laden asks a pertinent question: "For Mrs. Henley, and for women in the 18th century in general, are the two alternatives actually distinct?" Laden proposes that for these women there was "more similarity than difference between being 'happy and reasonable' and ceasing to be."[19] In the present discussion, it is important to examine the fate of Mrs. Henley in a different context, concentrating instead on the relationship between the form of the revelation of pregnancy and the form of the novel.

The disclosure of Mrs. Henley's pregnancy takes place in the shortest letter in the novel. It is also the penultimate letter, so that the announcement of one change in her condition is followed by the anticipation of another, more permanent change. She begins this letter by announcing, "I can no longer doubt it, my dear friend, I am with child" (36). The formulation of her announcement, referring as it does to the time preceding the writing of the letter, reflects a stylistic convention common to the epistolary novel: making the blank space between two missives delineate an event or change that took place between the time each one was written. Here, the blank stands for Mrs. Henley's initial suspicion and then certainty that she is with child. To begin the letter by indicating that this announcement is in fact belated reproduces what is an important aspect of pregnancy. The knowledge of pregnancy (and of the name of the father) is one area in which objective knowledge is always belated relative to woman's private knowledge of her body.[20] In fact, we learn that the letter comes very much after the moment when her intuition had suggested to her that she was to become a mother. Her friend is, in fact, number 3 on the list of people who have heard the good news. Mrs. Henley notes that she has already written to her aunt in London, and her aunt has already communicated the news to Mr. Henley, who is away from home at the moment. The details of this protagonist's disclosure, as it radiates outward from the solitary space of her writing to the public space of her husband's freedom, serve to delimit the boundaries of her agency. In light of our current understanding of the forces restricting women to the private sphere in late-eighteenth-century France, it is not surprising that this novel should present the bleakest future for the female protagonist, and not surprising that Mrs. Henley should end up staring vacantly into space, "I watch, and hours pass during which I have not thought even once about myself or my childish sufferings" (36).

In contrast to *Lettres de Mistriss Henley*, *Lettres neuchâteloises* (1784) presents a disclosure of a more public form. This second novel under consideration is a polyphonic epistolary novel, the plot of which concerns an apprentice, Henri Meyer, who becomes involved with two women. The first relationship is sexual and results in the pregnancy of Julianne, a tailor's assistant, whom he had met by accident. Of a more romantic nature, the second relationship begins as an awkward flirtation with a proper young woman, Marianne, and ends with the possibility of romance. Marianne is apparently intended for a happy fate, but Julianne is bought off and made to disappear after giving up her baby to Henri's uncle.

As a polyphonic epistolary novel, *Lettres neuchâteloises* has much less of the intimate, confessional quality so sought after in eighteenth-century women's fiction. That this text features instead the letters of five different correspondents is pertinent, for this genre, according to literary conventions, implies a more objective, less feminized, type of knowledge. Whereas in *Lettres de Mistriss Henley* the disclosure of the woman's pregnancy occurs in a letter to her female friend, in *Lettres neuchâteloises* the disclosure actually appears in a male character's letter to a male correspondent. In this letter, he describes a scene that features a woman assuming authority by speaking. But before the description of this scene, a letter from Julianne to her aunt hints at the problem. Wishing she had never met Henri, Julianne stoically asserts: "Il ne sert de rien de pleurer & de se lamenter quand il n'est plus tems; & si j'ai encore à pleurer, ce sera assez tems quand j'en serai sûre" (8:68–71) [It does no good to cry and to lament when it's too late, and if I have more to cry about there will be time enough when I am sure of it]. What Julianne refers to here is what is implied by the unfilled time before Mrs. Henley's disclosure: the woman's physical experience of reading her body for symptoms of pregnancy. This is Julianne's last letter. Henceforward, her speech is never cited directly and she is physically absent; the events connected with her pregnancy will be directed and reported by Marianne. Thus, one of the striking aspects of the disclosure in *Lettres neuchâteloises* is the absence of the mother. The reader learns, in Henri's letter to his uncle recounting how her pregnancy was revealed to him at a party, that Marianne has taken charge of Julianne's problem.[21] This revelation was orchestrated down to the smallest detail by Marianne, who arranges for Henri, his older male friend Max, and her to sit together and to behave in such a way as to conceal the fact that the three of them are involved in a serious conversation. Opening this conversation as the one in charge, Marianne warns Henri she must speak with him concerning "un chapitre qui devrait [m']être étranger" (79) [a matter that I shouldn't know anything about].

At this point it seems appropriate to speak of Marianne de la Prise's "prise de parole," a pun on her last name that combines both taking over and taking up a conversation. The elaborate construction of the context in which she will speak is so much more complicated than would be, for instance, an appropriate missive from Julianne. The novel does offer all the elements that would have been necessary for such a letter. It features two correspondents for Julianne: her aunt and Henri, either of whom could receive news of her pregnancy. Furthermore, from the content of her letters, we know that Julianne is not above asking Henri for money (earlier in the novel she had written to him for money to buy wood [56]) and that she is not afraid to commit to paper a potentially incriminating fact (she had written to her aunt that she was not a virgin [71]). Yet Charrière chose not to have Julianne write about her pregnancy. Admittedly, setting up Marianne to speak on Julianne's behalf, as

Charrière did for her all too fertile maid, Henriette Monachon, serves to mitigate the indecency of the unmarried girl's condition.[22] Furthermore, by putting the sinner in the background, attention can be focused on her condition as a problem to be solved. Within the context of Charrière's fiction, however, the way in which the revelation of pregnancy takes place in this novel sets up a point of comparison with *Lettres de Mistriss Henley*, because *Lettres neuchâteloises* also features the belatedness of the man's knowledge relative to that of the woman. In the latter, however, there is an additional component, for this belatedness is shown to put the man in a vulnerable position. Julianne knows; Marianne also knows. She deliberately withholds the news, keeping them in suspense while, for the purposes of deceiving onlookers at the party, permitting frequent interruptions. At one point they are interrupted by several women and, much to Henri's dismay, Marianne seats one of them next to her and begins chatting. "Imagine, si tu le peux, l'état où j'étois" (80) [Imagine, if you can, the state I was in] he complains to his male correspondent.

In fact, compared to the disclosure in *Lettres de Mistriss Henley*, where woman's expression is in the epistolary form traditionally associated with her, the disclosure of Julianne's pregnancy might look like a structure intended to empower Marianne as a speaking subject. Not only does she put Henri in a vulnerable position, she actually dominates both Henri and his friend. It is after they are sitting as she had instructed them that she asks if they are willing to do so, saying to Henri's friend as an afterthought. "Je n'ai pas attendu votre réponse" [I didn't wait for your answer] and only at this juncture asking Henri, "Monsieur, je ne vous ai point demandé si vous trouviez bon que je me mêlasse de vos affaires?" (80) [Sir, I have not asked you if you approve of my meddling in your affairs?] More seriously, it is only after she has revealed to Henri's friend that she will be addressing them out of "pitié pour une autre" [pity for another woman] (79), that Marianne asks Henri's consent to speak plainly in front of his friend, a man of a slightly higher social status than Henri. She remarks, "J'aurois dû vous le demander plutôt" (80) [I ought to have asked you this sooner], but her asking for his consent is purely rhetorical since she has just betrayed the nature of the secret about Henri.

We have seen that in both *Lettres de Mistriss Henley* and *Lettres neuchâteloises*, the primacy, relative to that of the man, of the woman's knowledge of her condition was built into the form of the disclosure. In the former, this primacy was merely implied by the blank space between two missives; in the latter, it assumed a greater significance and permitted a woman, although not the pregnant woman, to dominate the man who had engendered the baby. Equally significant is that in *Lettres de Mistriss Henley* the disclosure was made by the mother, writing from the confines of the private sphere, while in *Lettres neuchâteloises* it was made in a scene where one woman spoke on behalf of another in a public environment. Can this explain why the fate of the pregnant girl is presented as less tragic than the fate of the pregnant wife?[23] It is true that Julianne is put in a situation where she must, whether she wishes to or not, give up her baby; she is not, however, presented as having reached a state of suicidal despair.[24] The difference between these two novels suggests that in plotting the consequences for a woman of pregnancy, Charrière was able to sketch less negative consequences for her within the context of the genre that is not overdetermined as feminine by literary convention. From the idea that a greater emphasis on the female body may be linked to a decrease in the bleakness of her future, we might infer that this is pertinent to the significance of sexual difference in Charrière's fiction. The next text under consideration will confirm this.

With regard to the degree of privacy involved, the disclosure that Charrière presents in a later novel, *Trois femmes* (1798), is private to the extent that it involves only three women, but it is not private to the extent that the disclosure escapes the woman's control. Even more significantly, for the first time the focus is on pregnancy as a physical state rather than as knowledge of a physical state.

Written after the Terror, *Trois femmes* is one of those novels in which Charrière reflects upon the experiences of the aristocrats who fled from the bloodthirsty revolutionary government of France. The novel is narrated by the Abbé de la Tour, Charrière's pseudonym for a collection that includes four interconnected novels. It is in the novel featuring an almost omniscient narrator that the most positive outcome for the pregnant woman is chronicled. *Trois femmes* is in three parts. The plot of the first part, entitled *Trois femmes*, concerns Emilie, a young émigré exiled in Germany; her devoted maid, Josephine; and Constance, the wealthy widow who befriends them while recovering from the fortuitous carriage accident which deposited her at their door. The otherwise very pragmatic Josephine is also befriended, and perhaps even befuddled, by a

German manservant, who makes her pregnant. For her part, Emilie meets the boy-next-door, a German aristocrat, they fall in love, and are married. It is the story of Josephine's pregnancy that provides the continuity from the first part to the second: *Trois femmes, seconde partie*. Unlike those previously considered, in this novel the pregnant character does give birth. Furthermore, Josephine does not become suicidal like Mrs. Henley, nor does she give up her baby like Julianne. That it should be, of the three novels, the one in which the outcome for the woman will be the most positive, is of particular interest. The third part of *Trois femmes* (*Suite des Trois femmes*) consists mainly of a flashback that does not further the plot concerning Josephine's pregnancy but does further the implications of what control a woman has over her body.

In the other novels, Charrière has the pregnant woman announce that she is expecting, but here the disclosure literally bursts forth on its own. Emilie has noticed that Josephine seems depressed lately, and one day her beloved maid collapses, sobbing. The description that follows is striking. Josephine seems like she is about to suffocate, "quand Emilie coupant son lacet voit le cordon s'échapper comme un ressort subitement détendu, et son corset s'ouvrir du bas jusqu'au haut avec violence" (9:66) [when Emilie, cutting her corset, sees the lacing pop out like a spring suddenly released, and the corset open up violently from top to bottom]. The disclosure of pregnancy, then, is presented as a physical manifestation rather than as an act of speech. The focus on the physical is intensified when Emilie fails to comprehend what she is seeing and Josephine must enlighten her:

> Qu'est-ce? dit Emilie: qu'est-ce donc que vous avez, ma chère Josephine? Eh mon Dieu! ne le voyez-vous pas? dit Josephine. Est-ce à force d'indifférence ou à force de décence que vous ne voyez rien? Puis portant la main d'Emilie sur elle: à présent, dites, ignorez-vous encore ce que c'est? (67)

> ["What is it?" said Emilie. "What's wrong with you, my dear Josephine?" "Well, my god, don't you see?" said Josephine. "Is it through indifference or through prudishness that you see nothing?" Then, placing Emilie's hand on herself: "Now, tell me, do you still not know what it is?"]

It is significant that Josephine's interrogation proceeds from one physical sense (sight) to another (touch), as she resorts to tactile information in order to cure Emilie's "ignorance" of her condition. Presented in this way, knowledge about the baby is organized around the use of the senses. The emphasis on the physical here acquires a larger significance if we take into account Sigmund Freud's theory of social evolution. In the course of this evolution, paternity supplanted maternity, an event that he views as a victory of intellectuality over physicality. Freud takes as his premise the notion that humans may identify the mother through the simple use of their senses, but that to identify the father requires the exercise of a more intellectual nature (namely, hypothesizing who he is, based on the facts). He concludes that, as primitive humans became more advanced, they placed more importance on the intellectual than on the physical and so valued paternity over maternity. [25] For Freud, paternity is associated with the intellectual, maternity with the physical. The disclosure of pregnancy in *Trois femmes* might be understood as a vindication of maternity because it is constituted by the description of Emilie looking at and touching the body of the pregnant woman. More radically, if we take into account Luce Irigaray's appropriation or revision of Freud, *Trois femmes* figures a new interpretation of what woman means. Such a perspective will be treated further on in this chapter.

The emphasis on the physical is perpetuated in the course of an attempted elopement that puts Emilie's honor at risk. Alerted by a strange noise in the night, Josephine realizes that Emilie has been taken, willingly or not, and she runs to save her mistress:

> Elle est sortie ... et traversant trois jardins, franchissant divers obstacles comme elle l'eut fait au tem où sa taille étoit svelte et sa démarche légère, elle est arrivée ... tout auprès de la chaise de poste. (82)

> [She left the house ... and, crossing three gardens, vaulting different obstacles as she would have done in the time when her waist was svelte and her step light, she arrived ... right next to the carriage.]

The form of the description that Charrière gives of Josephine's intervention, an intervention which could have been handled in some other way (for example through her eavesdropping), evokes once again her pregnancy as a physical state rather than as a process that will produce a man's child. In the sequel to this text the value of the female body is presented even more explicitly.

With the consideration of *Trois femmes* we have progressed from a novel in which the disclosure of pregnancy was confessed by the protagonist (Mrs. Henley), to one in which the disclosure was narrated by a character (Henri), and finally to one in which the disclosure was recounted by an almost omniscient narrator. Using the working definitions proposed by Toril Moi, who distinguishes femininity, "a set of culturally defined characteristics," from biological femaleness and from political feminism, we could say that the less feminine the genre, the better the fate that may be plotted for the female character.[26] This correlation may in turn imply that the physical language of the female body entails a greater degree of empowerment for her than the conventional language of feminine fiction. The implications of the disclosures considered thus far are further elaborated through the role ascribed to the father in each novel.

The Role of the Father

Put quite bluntly, the way in which the man who engendered Mrs. Henley's child assumes his role as father proves destructive to the woman. When she broaches the subject of breastfeeding, her husband asserts the priority of his relationship to the child by stating simply that she will provide milk for his baby unless his friend, Dr. M, feels that the defects of Mrs. Henley's personality "indicated that a stranger would be preferable" (38). As Nadine Bérenguier has so convincingly shown, Mrs. Henley is as much a victim here of "recently introduced educational principles that deprived [women] of control over their own bodies" as she is of her unyielding spouse.[27] In a larger cultural context, Mrs. Henley as a woman reflects what Luce Irigaray identifies as the impulse by which man seeks to appropriate the power to give birth, the impulse to replace the umbilical cord by the phallus.[28] I would propose that Mrs. Henley is also a victim of genre, specifically of the type of fiction that both depended on and perpetuated woman's confinement to the private sphere. In the words of Janet Altman, "The spaces confining women writers ... dominat[ed] epistolary novels during the 17th and 18th centuries."[29] It is the monophonic epistolary novels — the paradigm of which is *Lettres portugaises*, appealing as it does to the concept of intruding into the intimacy of a woman's confession — that best embodies the repression of women in this way. With *Lettres de Mistriss Henley*, Charrière seems to push the genre to its limits deliberately, overconfining her female protagonist to the point where her existence is so diminished that it becomes the residue of an echo ("A note will inform you from time to time that your friend still lives until she no longer does"), and overconcentrating the novel to the point where it collapses in on itself ("After this [letter], I do not wish to write any more in this style" [36]). The conclusion of *Lettres de Mistriss Henley* makes it seem as if Charrière meant to kill off the genre along with her protagonist by making the moment when the protagonist's identity as woman becomes manifest coincide with the moment when her confinement to the private sphere becomes fatal. That the genre of the novel is indeed significant in this way is apparent in the following comparison.

The novel is organized so that in Mrs. Henley's last, almost lifeless letter, we learn that Mr. Henley had a bit of news he could have announced at the same time that his wife announced the news that she was expecting. Significantly, the masculine equivalent of Mrs. Henley's news is the news that her husband's refusal to become involved in public life will confine her to an even more restricted private life. As previously mentioned, Mr. Henley learned of his wife's condition from her aunt in London because he was not home at that moment. While in London, it seems, he was offered a seat in Parliament (41). Thus, at the moment when Mrs. Henley, at home, found herself in a position that is possible for women only, her husband, away from home, found himself in position that was possible for men only in the eighteenth century: he was invited to participate in the government. Setting up the news that Mr. Henley failed to announce to his wife as contemporaneous with the news that she *did* announce to him confirms the cultural significance of the gender "man" versus that of "woman" in the eighteenth century. In the social contract, as Carole Pateman explains, "all men, not just fathers, can generate political life and political right. Political creativity belongs not to paternity but masculinity."[30] The difference between the news Mr. and Mrs. Henley had to reveal to each other neatly defines masculine and feminine in this cultural context. It is reasonable that Mr. Henley failed to inform his wife of the offer that had been made to him. After all, of what concern could political matters be to a being whose identity is circumscribed by the private sphere?

The way in which Charrière presents what motivates Mr. Henley to tell his wife about this matter long after the fact is particularly revealing. Proceeding from the statement that he was away from home while she was at home, he lists first of all the difficulty of explaining himself in a letter (42), a genre at which women were considered to be naturally adept. Secondly, he states that she would not have succeeded in affecting his decision to decline the offer ("If you had objected your own reasons and tastes, I wouldn't have been shaken"), thereby excluding her, even in her capacity as his wife, from a matter related to the public sphere. Finally, Mr. Henley explains that he is telling her about the offer now because it has become a matter of public record. His statement delineates clearly his freedom of action and her confinement ("Had I not learned that the thing has become virtually public knowledge, you should never have known of either the proposal or the refusal" [42–43]). The order in which his reasons are presented marks the differences between their gendered roles and highlights her limited realm of agency.

After hearing her husband's belated announcement, Mrs. Henley surrenders to despair in her final missive, and Charrière conveys this wretched despair in stark words: "My situation is sad or else I am a being without reason or virtue" (37). Indeed, by the terms of the genre that the author was exploiting, woman was "a being without reason or virtue." Charrière's novel provides a fictional context in which we witness the atrophy and death of a woman who can no longer be a reflexive, writing individual once the meaning of her gender is determined by the significance that it has within the patriarchal social order: sexual reproduction. In addition, however, this determination of woman links the association of the monophonic, epistolary novel with the feminine.

While Mr. Henley may be said to have assumed too much authority over the child his wife was carrying, the father in *Lettres neuchâteloises* must be prodded into assuming any responsibility for the unborn child. Through the terms used by Henri in his announcement concerning Julianne's problem, a letter to his uncle in which he asks that his child be recognized in the event of his death, we can see the exactitude with which he defines his role in this matter.

Une jeune ouvrière, que je n'ai pas séduite, dit être grosse, & que je suis le père de son enfant: plusieurs circonstances, & *sur-tout la personne qu'elle a choisie pour cette confidence*, me persuadent qu'elle dit la vérité. (8:82; emphasis added)

[A young worker, whom I did not seduce, says that she's pregnant and that I'm the father of her child; several circumstances, and *especially the person that she chose for this confession*, convince me that she's telling the truth.]

Once again, as in the case of the initial disclosure, where Julianne did not speak, it is the role of Marianne as advocate that is validated. Henri's letter will precipitate the transfer of Julianne from Neuchâtel to his uncle's home in Frankfurt, a move that takes place at the speed of lightning. Henri's uncle writes, "Faites partir la fille" [Have the girl leave], to which his nephew replies, "La fille est partie" [The girl has left]. Julianne is to give up her baby to Henri's uncle, and then to disappear. In fact, this simply furthers the disappearance that had begun when Julianne's pregnancy became a factor and the letters stopped.

Like Mistress Henley, Julianne is in a position where she needs male support as a consequence of her pregnancy. In *Lettres de Mistriss Henley*, where the woman needed moral support from the man who engendered her child, she did not receive it. Instead, we have seen how Mr. Henley's appropriation of his wife's pregnancy led her to give up on life itself. In this instance, the woman needs financial support from the man who engendered her child, and she receives it. Perhaps, by having Julianne's pregnancy disclosed by another woman, Charrière created an outlet for Julianne that could not exist for Mrs. Henley, who was both the pregnant character and the narrator. While Julianne's letters stop once she discloses her pregnancy, at least her voice was taken up by another woman speaking on her behalf. In addition, this advocacy was effective to the extent that it ensured Julianne would receive what she needed from the father of the baby.

That Marianne's function as advocate is in fact what is pertinent in the episode of Julianne's pregnancy may be confirmed if we consider how her letters to her female friend change during the course of the novel. Before she becomes Julianne's spokeswoman, her letters are of a confessional nature. After the Julianne incident, which she does not confide to her correspondent, she writes in an assertive rather than confessional tone: "Je ne me trompois pas; [Henri] m'aime, cela est bien sûr; il m'aime" (86) [I was not mistaken; (Henri) loves me, that is very certain; he loves me]. It is her last letter that shows the most significant change. Responding to Henri's timid query about whether he is mistaken in thinking that she likes him, she answers simply, "Si vous vous étiez trompé, Monsieur, je serois fort embarrassée: mais pourtant je vous détromperois" (88) [If you were mistaken, Sir, I would be extremely embarrassed; but nonetheless I would undeceive you]. Whereas in the last letter to her female correspondent Marianne confirms that she was not in error, in this one-sentence letter to her male admirer Marianne sets herself up as the one with the knowledge to "undeceive" him. By continuing to assert herself as being in a position of power over knowledge relative to Henri, Marianne perpetuates the role that had been made possible for her though Julianne's choice of her as spokesperson. In *Lettres neuchâteloises*, woman's empowerment, made possible in the first place by exploiting the belatedness of the man's knowledge of the woman's pregnancy, makes the role of the father less destructive to the pregnant woman than it was in *Lettres de Mistriss Henley*.

Turning now to the next novel, we find the father in *Trois femmes* confronted by a woman, in a "role bien étrange pour elle" (69) [very strange role for her], speaking on behalf of the mother, just as was the case in *Lettres neuchâteloises*. In this novel, the father feels the weight of paternity even less than Henri Meyer did. This second Henri (the two characters have the same first name) already knows about the pregnancy, but he and Josephine disagree about what it means. Josephine thinks it means he must marry her because she says he is the father. Dismissing the possibility of finding a different husband, she explains that she cannot marry anyone else with "cet enfant dont Henri est le père" (9:68) [this baby whose father is Henri]. Henri does not want to marry her because he says he is not sure about being the father, given her loose morals. In the end, Emilie forces him to marry Josephine. The way in which the women arrange the marriage emphasizes the woman's right to say who the father of her child is and to claim authority over her body, just as the disclosure of the pregnancy in this novel had previously emphasized the woman's body. The principle underlying the representation of Josephine's pregnancy offers a sharp contrast to the negative description that Luce Irigaray gives of the childbearing tradition in the Western world. Referring to the man's desire to be the father, she writes that he "superimposes on the archaic world of flesh" a system of signification that wounds women, making "a hole in the belly of women," and deprives them of their identity.[31] The image of woman that Charrière gives us in Josephine is, on the contrary, an image by which power over this "archaic world of flesh" is reclaimed by woman, a world which, significantly, had to first break her corset in order to manifest itself.

The physical eloquence of Josephine's disclosure that she is pregnant and the diminution of the father's role in *Trois femmes* lead to the most positive outcome for the woman. In the light of the progression evident in the three novels studied here, a comparision of the fate charted for the three pregnant characters suggests that the greater the degree of control exercised by the woman over her body, the less negative her fate will be. The interpretation I am giving of Josephine's pregnancy will be confirmed by the rest of *Trois femmes*.

The Significance of Difference

In assessing what happens after the properly married Josephine gives birth, it is important to bear in mind that in eighteenth-century France the woman who gave birth to the baby was not necessarily the one who nursed or cared for it.[32] In Charrière's novel, we will see that she exploits the possibility of having the woman who gives birth to the baby not care for it. However, the episode of childbirth will be formulated in such a way as to be more than a reflection of French custom.

Before Josephine has her baby, Charrière introduces a secondary character, a countess, who is as pregnant as Josephine is. This means that both babies can be born at once and that they can be accidentally switched. While the midwife was attending to both mothers, the identically dressed babies (both of them male) were displaced in such a way that it became impossible to tell which was the aristocratic baby and which was the plebeian one.[33] At first glance it would seem that Charrière is doing nothing more than mixing up babies from different social classes. If the incident is seen in this light, it is, as Alix Deguise puts it, an ingenious way of proving the equality of all men.[34] This interpretation is consistent with the political ideals of Charrière. However, the incident takes on a different meaning insofar as it contributes to the coherence of a text in which there appears a statement about sexual difference — namely, Constance's previously mentioned commentary. The aftermath of this episode suggests that what is being considered here is the nature of the mother rather than the status of the child. Indeed, the baby boys are baptized with the same name, further increasing the similarity between them. At the same time, however, the mothers become even more dissimilar. In the end, the mothers in this novel reflect an unusual distribution of maternity, as the two mothers with one baby each are ultimately integrated into an assortment of three different kinds of mothers.

The aristocratic mother, the countess, at first believes that she will recognize her offspring when it manifests its noble blood. However, she is quickly disgusted by both screaming infants and, losing interest in motherhood, becomes the mother of none. For her part, Josephine is happy to nurse both of "ces deux équivoques enfans" (114) [these two equivocal children], as Constance puts it, and she becomes the mother of two. To complicate further the representation of maternity, Constance, who has not been pregnant, becomes a once-removed mother of two when she takes over the responsibility for the orphaned boy and girl on whom she will conduct her gender experiment described at the beginning of this chapter.

If we considered only the countess who abandoned her baby and the lower-class woman, Josephine, who undertook to nurse this baby in addi-tion to her own, we would have no more than the representation of wet nursing in eighteenth-century France. However, the integration of three different maternal roles into the childbirth episode exceeds this context. In addition, when we take into account what happens to pregnant women in the other novels, the idea that Josephine should keep her baby and even acquire another becomes crucial. Only in *Trois femmes* does the pregnant character have the chance to choose to appropriate her baby; in the other novels, she is dispossessed of it. Mistriss Henley, upon realizing that her husband considered her to be nothing more than the nest of his all-important child, lost interest in the pregnancy and longed for death. In *Lettres neuchâteloises,* Julianne was paid to give her baby over to her seducer's uncle and to disappear forever. Clearly, Josephine is the char-acter who comes out ahead — and she is the only one whose pregnancy was represented in a physical description of the woman's body.

The most pertinent factor in assessing the episode of the two displaced babies is the role of Constance's experiment because it is explicitly designated as "la petite pièce" (114) [the codicil] to the episode. The gender experiment lends a particular significance to the maternal roles assumed by the countess, Josephine, and Constance because it provides a motivation for the commentary on sexual difference in which Constance reiterates the ideas proposed by the Englishman in "Lettre d'un Anglois." It should be noted that while the Englishman merely suggested that the "faculties" of women and men "are very similar in one and the other sex," Constance devises a scientific experiment to prove it. Having her experiment designated as the "codicil" to the baby-switching incident confirms that what is important here is not the status of the two babies who were accidentally switched but the variety of the mothers who were thus engendered: by this I mean that Charrière is assigning a particular meaning to gender here. By presenting child raising as a choice rather than a consequence of the female body, she frees woman's body from the social constraints that an essentialist interpretation of her body can impose on her.

The seduction, pregnancy, and childbirth that Josephine experiences take up the first two parts of *Trois femmes*. Thus far, the representation of woman's natural difference may be summed up in the distinction that Charrière's novel makes between childbearing and child raising. Although the female body is distinctive in its capacity for childbearing, it is not distinctive in its function for child raising; the woman who abandons her infant is as female as the one who appropriates it. The consequences of this freedom from being defined by the body are explored in the sequel, *Suite des trois femmes*. Published separately after Charrière's death, this sequel sets up Constance with a motive to tell her life story, *Histoire de Constance*.[35] The character who reiterates the Englishman's assertion that the physical differences between men and women are of no importance receives a history that lends greater complexity to the treatment of this issue. Constance's past provides the negative complement to the implications of gender neutrality presented earlier in *Trois femmes*.

Histoire de Constance chronicles the genesis of this provocative character who recounts why she decided to never fall in love. By way of explanation, she tells a tragic story, but it is not the story of Constance's own love affair. Instead, she recounts her uncle's love affair with a woman in Martinique. Plotting this love affair in Martinique allows Charrière to represent a heroine who is a black slave. Constance explains that the slave was named Bianca "par plaisanterie" (147) [as a joke], so this black woman literally embodies difference. Bianca was, of course, exceptionally beautiful, and she was off limits to everyone except her owner, an elderly woman, who concealed Bianca. One day, however, the woman's nephew, Victor, catches sight of her standing in a white marble enclosure with water up to her waist. She is black, she is a slave, she is absolutely different. He falls in love. Despite a feeling on the part of all concerned that it will not turn out well, Victor takes Bianca to his property and sets her up as his mistress. The premonitions of doom are justified when a troop of comedians comes to town and two actresses captivate Victor. As in so many of Charrière's novels, the man is too passive to help the woman he loves in any way. Although Victor realizes that by neglecting Bianca for the actresses, and by tolerating their abusive treatment of her, he is breaking her heart, he does not act.[36] When she begs him to send her back to his aunt before disaster strikes, he refuses and thereby brings about the disaster.[37]

In what is one of the most shocking scenes in Charrière's fiction, she describes Bianca, "furieuse et désesperée" (150) [furious and desperate], wandering around the house in the middle of the night. The woman enters her lover's room, coming through the window with a knife in her hand, and lunges forward. She raises the knife. Unfortunately, Victor wakes up and summons help. The servants subdue Bianca and tie her up, despite Victor's protests. Later, the judges find her guilty of attempted murder, despite Victor's claim that she is with child. Bianca resolutely rejects the pregnancy defense.[38] Charrière's character refuses to seek refuge in woman's capacity to bear children. She dismisses all of Victor's efforts on her behalf, saying: "J'ai toute ma raison; qu'on m'emmene; j'ai voulu faire une action juste mais je n'en dois pas moins etre punie et ne demande qu'une prompte mort" (151) [I am perfectly sane; take me away. I wanted to accomplish a just action, but I must nonetheless be punished and ask only for a prompt death]. For the attempted murder of her lover and the father of her child, a man who had become her tyrant (149), she is executed.

It makes sense for Charrière to add depth to a character such as Constance, the woman responsible for a gender-switching experiment on orphaned twins, by detailing the significance to her of Bianca's story. The interpretation that Constance derives from her uncle's love story is perfectly gender neutral. Concluding that *both* men and women can behave badly in a relationship, Constance decides never to fall in love, fearful that she might behave like either Victor or Bianca. In the context of the novel as a whole, however, Bianca's story is more than just the reason Constance will never fall in love. Situated as the sequel to the childbirth episode, which implies that women are free to choose or decline child raising, Bianca's story provides the corollary to the principle inherent in this freedom. Because Bianca refused the special protection of pleading pregnancy, her acceptance of the death penalty is not just a way for the seduced and abandoned woman to commit suicide;

it is a way for the woman who is absolutely different to be treated absolutely the same. Only by demanding to be treated no differently than a man does this woman acquire what she has never had: the right to be treated as if her nonwhite, enslaved, and misnamed body did not determine her status in society. The frighteningly stark doctrine illustrated here would today be called gender neutrality.

A brief digression is in order here to comment on the last of the novels in the collection that Charrière published under the pseudonym of the Abbé de la Tour, because of the way in which pregnancy is featured. *Les Ruines de Yedburg* (1799) is hardly her most well crafted work, but in it she created a female character, Jenny Southwell, who is compelling if only because she is so nasty. While the main point of the plot is to illustrate the idea that sometimes people are best left uneducated and even poor, the subplot concerns Jenny's scheme to claim she is pregnant in order to force the young man of her choice to marry her. The daughter of "une femme intéressée et méchante" [a nasty, self-serving woman], Jenny is described as "perverse" (9:328 and 335). The means by which she lays the foundation for her claim are not presented in the novel: "Beaucoup d'artifices furent employés. Ils réussirent" (335) [Many deceitful maneuvers were used. They worked]. The scene pitting Jenny and her mother against the young man, Charles, and his uncle foregrounds the ruthlessness of the two women, and it is interrupted by a valet, in the role of a *deus ex machina*, who bursts in to display a purloined letter proving that Jenny's claim is nothing more than a plot to get Charles. Because Jenny threatens not only a lawsuit but an ongoing barrage of harassment directed at his family, Charles surrenders and gives her his last name. She never has a child and instead wanders around after a suitably despicable fellow with whom she is eventually discovered in a position that requires no explanation (342). Charles divorces her. In the end, all the characters in *Les Ruines de Yedburg* are left in varying degrees of unhappiness.

While pregnancy in this text is only a threat, not a reality of the woman's body as it was in *Trois femmes*, this plot further elaborates the notion that pregnancy does not qualify as "special circumstances." Here it is but one of the various reprehensible aspects of this unpleasant woman. Interestingly enough, this novel, which is the only one of Charrière's novels to feature a false claim of pregnancy — a menace unique to women — also features the only occurrence in Charrière's fiction of another menace, one that is unique to men: the threat of a duel (343). While it is true that only a woman could threaten to make trouble by claiming that a particular man made her pregnant, only a man in the eighteenth century could threaten to make trouble by challenging another man to a duel. Evil characters of each sex have at their disposal a special threat that they can make. Woman's ability to lay the charge of paternity at the door of an innocent man happens to be a function of her body, but it is not "special" if it is seen in terms of an equivalence between man and woman, just as being a woman does not make a would-be murderer "special."

The black slave named Bianca, "as a joke," provides a necessary supplement to what is implied by Josephine's pregnancy in the first part of *Trois femmes*. Charrière's series of differing maternities presents her argument that woman's physical difference alone, as manifested through a function unique to her body, does not define her. Indeed, this is precisely what Constance, and before her the fictional Englishman, advocated. Adding strength to their argument is the price that women must pay when they are defined in essentialist terms, as illustrated so vividly in *Lettres de Mistriss Henley*. Her pregnancy is the occasion for her husband to reduce her to the status of unthinking womb. The beginnings of a way out of such a dead end are sketched in *Lettres neuchâteloises*, where the possibility of woman's empowerment is depicted. It is only in *Trois femmes* that the context for realizing this possibility is fully outlined. But the terrible emancipation achieved by Bianca must be factored into the implications of freedom from difference, or else this is only a partial freedom. From her death we may derive the unsentimental view that the principle of gender neutrality, although a valid principle, can have chilling results.

The contextualization in Charrière's novel *Trois femmes* of a statement privileging gender equality over sexual difference offers a way of rethinking the status quo by the terms of which "inequality comes first; difference comes after," as MacKinnon puts it. Physical difference, inscribed in the representation of Josephine's pregnancy, does not "determine anything whatsoever relative to our intellectual faculties," as Constance puts it. While in the image of Mistress Henley and of Julianne we see only difference translated into inequality, in that of Josephine we can see true difference. We must note that Constance makes her speech only *after* the disclosure of Josephine's pregnancy and the results of childbirth have been presented in such a way as to restore authority over the woman's body to the woman. The principle that Constance expresses may be described as "gender *ed* neutrality." This principle, recognizing and respecting woman's embodied existence, would entitle her to freedom from the special protection that perpetuates her inferior status. Reflecting upon such respect for difference in an alternative social order, Margaret Homans points to the vastness of the changes that would have taken place: "The symbolic order, with its phallic priority and its denigration of women, would have ceased as well."[39] Such was not the case in late-eighteenth-century society, and it is certainly not the case now.

As feminists today, we face medical controversies that foreground woman's physical differences from man, and they are posed by a medical technology of which the eighteenth century could not have dreamed.[40] The position taken by Irigaray is that we urgently need a gendered social and cultural ethic.[41] She writes of the need to bring about economic parity between the sexes — an ideal, however, that is meaningless without a parallel recognition of women as women. This recognition should not make of women men with handicaps, such as pregnancy, but should take into account in a positive way what is particular to them. Irigaray advocates a legal definition of "woman" as virgin and potentially mother in order to enforce recognition by the law of woman's right to control her body.[42] The worlds of *Trois femmes*, with Josephine's unexpected child/children and Constance's radical opinions about the difference between men and women, together illustrate what I have called gendered neutrality, and seem surprisingly close to these ideals. Once authority over the woman's body is recognized as hers, there is no need for special protection.

5

Belle / Agnès / Zélide / Madame de Charrière

What might knowing the life story of Isabelle de Charrière contribute to feminism today? Answering this question entails a reflection on biography, a genre around which one of the tensions in feminism today crystallizes. According to one school of thought, we need to develop an appreciation of woman that is based on her true nature, one that can counter the negative, masculinist interpretations prevalent in our culture. Another school of thought advocates instead utilizing deconstruction as a means of eliminating any theoretical validity of "Woman" as an absolute. In the context of this ongoing debate, biography is particularly tantalizing; it holds out an inviting promise to "conve[y] the relevancies of its small slice of then for the now its readers are living," in the succinct formulation of Liz Stanley.[1] Biography might provide both a corrective and a contribution to feminist theory. Not only can it serve, in principle, to make known what was historically considered secondary and marginal — namely, the material consequences of living as a woman — it may contribute to changing standards by which women today view their life.[2] A worthwhile endeavor, but one can also claim the genre may be dangerous to the feminist cause. On the one hand, it can be argued that biography is flawed by the implications that all women are determined by a common nature transcending the distinctions of race, class, and sexual orientation. On the other hand, feminists for whom deconstruction has proven to be a useful working concept may claim that what has traditionally been the very aim of biography, to present in some unambiguous form a unified self, living or dead, is complicitous with sexism. For these theorists, the unified self is one of the building blocks of sexism, serving to imprison the female subject in an identity from which she cannot escape.

Currently, feminist biographers like Sharon O'Brien are searching for ways out of this theoretical impasse. She advocates creating life stories that will satisfy both types of requirements: to transmit "many female voices and stories" while respecting the significance of other aspects of identity such as class, race, and sexual preference, and to realize the goals of deconstruction by refusing to perpetuate the myth of the totalizing, unified self transparently accessible through historical documentation.[3] The complexity of this challenge is apparent in her provocative assessment of her own biography of Willa Carther: O'Brien states point blank that she "never intended to deliver the real Willa Carther to the reader."[4] What then can a feminist biography offer us? It can offer the appeal and satisfaction of storytelling in any narrative form that demonstrates the complexity of woman's experience and identity while engaging the theoretical debate outlined above.

What is presented in this chapter is also not meant to produce the "real" Charrière, and so it is by no means a full-length biography of Charrière for several reasons. This is in part because two new biographies of her have just been published and in part because the extent of such a task would detract from what has been my focus in this study.[5] The main reason, however, for not undertaking such a project is the image Charrière gives us of herself in her early self-portrait, "Zélide," an image contesting the idea that a text could encompass a woman's self. However, the Isabelle de Charrière presented here is intended to engage the issues raised by feminist biography. To this end, the discussion is organized around two different poles. In the first section, the focus is on Charrière's lived experience. From one segment of her correspondence, the letters concerning her pregnant maid, I propose to derive a "small slice of then" that pertains to one woman's experience confronting her society over a woman's issue: pregnancy out of wedlock. Organized around a different approach, deconstruction, the focus of the second section addresses the text of "Zélide" (1763–64). The form of the self it articulates delineates a paradigm for conceiving woman's identity in a way that is not repressive. The deliberately fragmented totality that emerges from this two-part reading — Isabelle (Belle) Agneta (Agnès) Elisabeth van Tuyll van Serooskerken van Zuylen / Madame de Charrière — is a more suitable figure for this author than the image perpetuated in the tradition of Charrière biography: the difficult young girl who became an unhappy wife writing novels in a small town.

Gendered Experience I

The standard biography of Charrière (1740–1805) runs as follows. Born into a large aristocratic family of the Netherlands, Belle (short for Isabelle) was destined to be difficult to marry off, or so it would seem. In the first biography of her, the two-volume *Madame de Charrière et ses amis* (1906), Philippe Godet sums up the problem as follows:

Elle n'a jamais consenti à paraître ce que le monde, ou les conventions sociales, ou les préjugés des pédants et des sots, auraient souhaité qu'elle fût.... D'où le conflit qui éclate dès sa prime jeunesse entre elle et le milieu où elle grandit.[6]

[She never consented to appear what the world, or social conventions, or the narrow-minded judgment of pedants and fools, would have wished that she be.... Hence the conflict that erupts from her earliest youth between her and the milieu in which she grew up.]

At the age of twenty-two, she met an older man, David-Louis Constant d'Hermenches, a military man. Although this was improper, they began a correspondence that would last sixteen years. That in 1991 these letters should be collected by Isabelle Vissière and Jean-Louis Vissière into an anthology (more than six hundred pages in length) entitled *Une Liaison dangereuse*, bears witness to the persistence with which this relationship has served to categorize Charrière.

The increasingly desperate search for a spouse for the unconventional young woman ended when she married Charles-Emmanuel de Charrière at the age of thirty-one.[7] They moved to Neuchâtel. Living the life of an intelligent, married, childless woman in a provincial environment, Charrière launched her literary career. Or, to view her life as Geoffrey Scott did in his 1926 essay: "The society on the shores of the lake feared her and starved her mind.... Madame de Charrière lived, gallantly, in a perpetual void. Stoically, she sought to fill it by a ceaseless activity of the mind and pen."[8] Her literary output began with *Lettres neuchâteloises* and *Lettres de Mistriss Henley*. The latter was commonly read as a veiled description of her marriage. The image of her as a bright, intelligent woman married to a dull man is the image that Simone de Beauvoir gives of her in *Le Deuxième Sexe*. After discussing the recent case of a forty-year-old woman who had simply one day strangled her "mari odieux,"

Beauvoir goes on to present the case of Charrière, using her to illustrate the idea that marriage suffocates women.[9] Although this interpretation is misguided because it is based on Scott's impressionistic biography, Beauvoir's reading of him does serve to show the extreme uses to which the life story of Charrière may be put.[10]

Charrière encountered Benjamin Constant in 1787 and would maintain a relationship with him, punctuated by periods of antagonism and silence, until her death. For literary history, the result of the Charrière/Constant relationship was to make of this woman, "une des humanistes les plus remarquables du XVIIIe siècle" [one of the most remarkable humanists of the eighteenth century], a mere footnote in the history of the male author.[11] Their relationship has been interpreted as an older woman/younger man relationship disrupted by the arrival on the scene of the younger Mme de Staël. The most extreme and virulent version of this scenario is to be found in Anthony West's *Mortal Wounds*. According to West, upon meeting Constant, the forty-seven-year old Charrière "saw at once that he was the child she might have had by d'Hermenches and that he was desperately in need of love and understanding," an interpretation that would seem to suggest almost an incestuous aspect to the relationship.[12] Seven years later, "when Madame de Staël met Constant ... she was twenty-eight, and she was without sexual inhibitions of any kind: that Madame de Charrière would lose him to her was inevitable" (219). However, in a study of their correspondence, Isabelle Vissière argues convincingly against this cliché, stating categorically that the split between them was of a political nature.[13] Constant's claim, reported in *Le Cahier rouge*, that Charrière had had an affair with a younger man has been erected into some sort of myth about the matter, a myth confirming the image of this bright intellectual woman, stifled in marriage, unfulfilled outside of it. From such a mytho-biography we can learn only that intelligent women cannot be happy in marriage, and unhappy women write a lot. Underlying this, of course, is the answer to Freud's question: "What does a woman really want?" In sum, what the biography of Charrière presents us is what we have projected onto it, whether it be panegyric (Godet), misogynistic (Scott and West), or feminist (Beauvoir). The following two points of comparison provide telling evidence of this.

In Godet's biography, a biography that begins, "Voilà vingt ans que j'aime madame de Charrière" [For twenty years now I have loved

Madame de Charrière], he tackles the question of whether she was pretty or not. Referring to the bust that Jean-Antoine Houdon sculpted of her, Godet judges both Houdon's execution of his project and the model for it to be "infiniment spirituel," yet cautions that the sculpture "n'autorise guère à parler de 'beauté" (1:181) [does not justify speaking of beauty]. He concludes that she was neither pretty nor beautiful: she was "charming." It was two years later that West selected Charrière, along with Germaine de Staël and Georges Sand, for the behavioral study he presented in *Mortal Wounds*, aiming to show "the very direct way in which the content of their work was determined by the forces that dictated their behavior" (vii). The chief driving force he attributes to these women is "large demands of love denied in early life." His treatment of the bust by Houdon is remarkably unlike Godet's. Addressing the question of whether Charrière did or did not try to make her husband become more spontaneous in his love making, West decides that she probably did not, adducing as particularly significant the "evidence" of the Houdon bust. "It is very obvious from this that the sculptor was repelled by his subject, to whom he gave the face of a cold, bloodless, and frightened young man, whose expression suggests that he is contemplating some disagreeable prospect" (205). West has changed the gender of the bust and attributes to it a gaze that might more properly be considered his own.

The different presentations given of the extramarital affair in which Charrière was supposedly involved provide an even more provocative point of comparison. Comparing the description given by Scott and Beauvoir, we find that, in Scott's words, Charrière was seeking "an outlet for the locked riches of her nature" when she "fell disastrously in love with an insignificant and handsome individual at Geneva, an episode which ended in humiliation and despair" (xiii–xiv). In Beauvoir's words, "Un jeune homme traversa sa vie, brièvement, et la laissa plus seule encore qu'auparavant" (319) [a young man crossed her path, briefly, and left her even more alone than before].[14] While both critics focus on the destructive aspects of the relationship, Scott's version shows Charrière being diminished by the experience while Beauvoir's version depicts her as being merely restored to a previous state.[15]

In order to decide what we can say about the author we know today as Isabelle de Charrière, we must confront the material reality of the novels, political treatises, plays, musical scores, and correspondence that together make up the ten volumes of her *Oeuvres complètes*.[16] With regard to the author of fiction that pertains so directly to feminism today, the older mytho-biography that has such a grip on perceptions of Charrière is no longer appropriate. The current context of this author's fiction requires elaborating a different perspective from which to view her life. One of the recommendations O'Brien makes concerning feminist biography is that we pay attention to "the possibility that the female subject may occupy many 'subject positions' in a life."[17] With that in mind, the following alternative to the mytho-biography sketched above aims to displace the status previously accorded to her relationships with men. The change in perspective effected is significant. By supplying a needed adjustment, such a change can point to a different, feminist, perspective on her life.

Gendered Experience II

Instead of viewing Charrière as the rejected bride of many suitors, a more meaningful image of her may emerge if we privilege her woman-centered relationships, As Jackson warns in her reading of Charrière's friendship with Isabelle de Gélieu: "It is not always easy to deprogram the conditioned reflex whereby we subordinate the dynamics of female friendship to those of heterosexual involvement and even ascribe to that involvement a monopoly on eventfulness."[18] Undertaking to "reprogram our reflexes" when viewing her life will lessen the hold of previous narratives concerning Charrière. Mention of an early relationship, the one with her Genevan governess, Jeanne-Louise Prevost (1721–85), will serve as a point of departure. Next, and more importantly, a detailed account of the relationship she had with her pregnant maid, Henriette Monachon (1766–[?]) will depict one of the significant experiences of Charrière's life.

Charrière's mother, orphaned at the age of twelve, was only sixteen years old when she gave birth to Isabelle (the first of seven children), so it may be that her governess was especially important to the young girl. Certainly the letters of Prevost written after she had left her post in 1753 (for reasons of ill health) seem to indicate a close relationship between the young girl and her governess, even considering the extent to which personal letter writing then was a stylized genre. However, because the letters of Isabelle have not been preserved, I will not dwell on this correspondence. Instead I would like to propose, as an exercise, seeing in the author we know today as Isabelle de Charrière a woman who was strongly influenced in her youth by her intellectual relationship with a woman of a lower class. It was after all Prevost who introduced Isabelle to French, the language that would eventually supplant her own native tongue, and to travel: in 1750, Isabelle visited Switzerland and France with her. A focus on her relationship with Prevost would thus privilege her experience of and empathy for French culture. In this Charrière it is easy to recognize the one who, at the age of forty-eight, had such a lucid view of her homeland and its politics. In the previously cited letter to her brother Vincent, she sketches an insightful comparison of her feelings toward the Netherlands and France:

> En preferant à certains egards ma nation à *toute autre*, oui à toute autre ... je n'aime point du tout mon paijs. Un sol humide, un *republique* asservie me deplaisent à l'excès: [et] je suis prevenue pour la france.... C'est leur langue que je parle le mieux c'est leur livres que je connois le mieux c'est avec eux que je suis le plus à mon aise; C'est leur heroïsme quand ils en ont qui me seduit le plus. (3:92; emphasis in the original)

> [While preferring in some ways my nation (the Netherlands) to *any other*, yes, to any other ... I don't like my country at all. A humid ground, a servile *republic* displease me no end; (also) I am biased in favor of France.... It is their language that I speak the best, it is their books that I know the best, it is with them that I am most comfortable. It is their heroism, when they have it, that seduces me the most.]

During her lifetime, Charrière's spiritual French-ness would lead to her eventual integration into a vast network of correspondents commenting on contemporary events. (In her *Oeuvres complètes,* the correspondence alone takes up six volumes, and Isabelle Vissière goes so far as to compare Charrière's epistolary empire to that of Voltaire.[19]) This was, of course, a period in European history when such francophone tendencies were essential to anyone who aspired to be cultured or even literate, and so it could be argued that Charrière merely followed a trajectory common among the educated classes. Nonetheless, the idea of continuity between the two Charrières — the young Isabelle, aged thirteen to eighteen, who corresponded in French with her ex-governess, and the author represented in six volumes of correspondence — may counter the weight accorded to her marriage/marital problems as indicators of her inner self.

Turning now to a relationship that flourished during her writing years (or, rather, that agitated them), I read the correspondence involving mention of Charrière's controversial maid Henriette Monachon, a young woman who became pregnant out of wedlock not once but twice. The relevant letters, more than one hundred sixty of them, cover the period 25 May 1791 to 27 May 1801. Why Henriette? She is a figure pertinent to a feminist perspective on Charrière's life because the pregnant maid is a person deemed inferior by society, as was woman in general in eighteenth-century France, and because she boldly manifests woman's physical difference from man through her unrepentant pregnancies. When, with her husband's permission, Charrière took up the defense of her maid, she committed herself to a cause of particular significance to women, as evident in her statement four months before the birth of Henriette's first bastard: "Quand je compare seche pruderie, habitude sale & egoiste, Coeur glacé, precautions depravées, & grossesse c'est à grossesse que je donne la preference" (letter to Caroline de Sandoz-Rollin, 7 January 1792; 3:330) [When I compare dry prudishness, dirty and egotistical habits, frozen heart, depraved precautions, and pregnancy, it is pregnancy that I favor]. Contrasting "dry prudishness" and simple pregnancy in this way restores pregnancy to woman, detaching it from its attendant social regulation, a gesture that anticipates the scenario Charrière will create for Emilie, Constance, and Josephine with regard to the unplanned pregnancy in *Trois femmes*. What emerges through her letters concerning Henriette is the painful transformation of this woman from an abstract principle of importance to an all too real, all too difficult human being. In effect, these letters tell a story about the perils of undertaking a feminist cause in a patriarchal society.

Pertinent models for reading a correspondence have been proposed by, among others, Susan Jackson and Elizabeth MacArthur. In her study of the Charrière/Gélieu letters previously mentioned, Jackson refers to the paradigm of the doctor/patient relationship.[20] She analyzes the rhetoric of this relationship as it is used by the two Isabelles to mark fluctuations in the relationship. Drawing her approach from a more literary source, MacArthur reads both real and fictional correspondences according to a revised concept of metaphor and metonomy.[21] While these critics are not making explicitly feminist claims, such models are pertinent to experimentation with feminist biography, for in the privilege they assign to language, the idea of a unified self is devalued without devaluing attentiveness to the lived experience of the female authors considered. To assess the letters about Henriette according to similar principles, I read the Henriette created by Charrière as a figment of her imagination, or, put less simplistically, I trace the evolution in the descriptions Charrière gives of Henriette over the course of their changing relationship. From the maid's image we may infer the history of Charrière's own experience. There are four stages in the relationship between Charrière and Henriette. In the first stage, parallels between Henriette and her mistress are emphasized, so Henriette signifies more through her similarity to Charrière than through her own qualities. In the second, she has more personal qualities and seems like a sister. The relationship is at its most intense in the third stage, characterized as it is by the tension between Charrière's feelings for her maid and the overpowering social pressure to abandon her; during this period the image given of Henriette vacillates from one extreme to another. Finally, in the fourth stage, the relationship dissolves and Henriette is presented rather surprisingly as a stereotype: a whore.

Henriette had been Charrière's maid for over three years before the author mentions her. In a letter to her friend Caroline de Sandoz-Rollin (25 May 1791), Charrière refers to Henriette's seduction, manifesting some sympathy for the girl (3:297–98). Paradoxically, it is only when Henriette is later pregnant, an experience her mistress never had, that she not only sympathizes with her but identifies with her. While in her first letter about Henriette, Charrière had presented her as a tabula rasa — "Rien n'annonce de l'ame ni de la raison" (298) [Nothing suggests either a soul or an intelligence] — in the letter discussing Henriette's pregnancy, Charrière focuses on the similarities between them. She lists Henriette's brusqueness, her impatience, and the exaggeration with which she "aprecie, sent, exprime chaque chose" [judges, feels, expresses everything].

J'ai une grande indulgence pour les defauts d'Henriette Monachon ... cela non seulement parce qu'elle m'est dailleurs très agreable mais aussi parce qu'elle me ressemble dans toutes ces choses là & que je crois devoir expier avec elle ce que j'ai fait souffrir à d'autres par ces mêmes defauts plus inexcusables en moi qu'en elle vu la diference de nos educations. (3:329)

[I am very indulgent with regard to the flaws of Henriette Monachon ... and that not only because she otherwise is very appealing to me, but also because she is like me in all those ways and I feel I must expiate with her what I impose on others through these same flaws, flaws that are more inexcusable in me than in her, given the difference in our education.]

These similarities reappear in a letter to her brother, Vincent, but they are implicit. Regarding Henriette's refusal to name the father of her baby, Charrière compares it to the girl's silence during the period of her seduction — "Mais celle qui se tait si à propos s'est aussi tue mal à propos" (3:331) [But she who is so very right to remain silent was also very wrong to remain silent] — and then goes on to refer to the hostility that she herself encountered as a result of defending her pregnant maid: "On la deteste assez universellement ... & cela parce que je l'aime ... voilà ou le silence eut été bon & fort à sa place" [She is more or less universally detested ... and that because I like her.... There's where silence would have been very much in order]. The similarity can even become equality. Responding to Constant's charge that people of Charrière's class "devour" lower-class people, she uses Henriette to illustrate the give and take that structures her relationship to lower-class people:

Est-ce donc que je les mange quand je les nourris les caresse & les amuse; et elles doivent-elles me mordre & y a t-il apparence qu'elle me mordent? *Je vous ai Henriette*: lui disois-je avant hier. *Moi j'ai madame* me repondit-elle. (3:363; emphasis in original)

[Am I then eating them when I nourish, caress, and entertain them? And ought they to bite me, and is there any evidence that they bite me? *I have you, Henriette*, I was saying to her the day before yesterday. *Me, I have madame*, she answered me.]

That her emphasis on similarity should develop into an implied equality reflects a component of her political philosophy. Charrière's belief in class distinctions was far from committed; she felt they were practical, and she had a sentimental fondness for the ideal of nobility. To see her political philosophy reflected in the descriptions she gives of Henriette reveals the extent to which the maid, at this point, functioned as an abstract principle in Charrière's perspective. The hold exercised by this principle on her led her to flaunt the social condemnation of out-of-wedlock pregnancy. Indeed, Charrière set herself up as the champion of Henriette's cause. In her letter to Jean-Piere de Chambriere d'Oleyres, she states bluntly that today, "en dépit des mechans, des prudes des sots, des inclemens" [despite mean, prudish, foolish, reluctant people], she is personally having baptized a child whose father is unspecified and she is taking back into her home and service the mother of this problematic child (3:355). Here Charrière puts into action her stated principle that pregnancy is more worthy than "dry prudishness." This first stage of the Charrière/Henriette relationship ends victoriously, and in summing up the episode, Charrière lays claim to what she has created. Writing to Henriette L'Hardy (7–8 May 1792), she asserts that Henriette is guilty of "une *faute*," not of a crime, and she concludes significantly that "mon Henriette" [my Henriette] and her child are both doing well (359).

The second stage of this dynamic relationship, a brief period of tranquillity in between the two pregnancies of Henriette, is marked by greater equality between the two women. The tone for this second stage is set by a letter to Henriette L'Hardy (14 August 1792) in which Charrière virulently condemns someone who had insulted Henriette (3:403). References to the confidence that Charrière has in Henriette's judgment are consistent during this period; for example, with regard to the family problems of another maid, Charrière writes that Henriette is her "oracle" in such matters (3:469), thus elevating Henriette even above equal rank with her mistress.[22] Two other maids are seduced during this time, which provides a means for assessing the intensity of Charrière's attachment to Henriette. We will see that now she goes beyond claiming that Henriette was guilty only of an error. Concerning the experience of seduction, Charrière sets up two different points of comparison for Henriette. In her mention of Lisette, who is trying to avoid an admirer, Charrière goes on at length about Henriette's empathy and her willingness to counsel the young girl (3:586). The remark about Lisette's problem serves to further exculpate Henriette with regard to her own seduction. Later, referring to Rosette, who is suspected of being pregnant, Charrière confesses simply that she has less sympathy for Rosette than she had had for Henriette because

l'indulgé & l'indulgent sont ce qu'ils sont d'après des circonstances des convenances des manieres d'être particulieres & non generales; & qu'elle et moi ne pouvons rien pour telle & telle autres personnes. (4:25)

[the indulged one and the one who is indulgent are what they are as a result of circumstances, arrangements, particular and not general ways of being; and she and I can do nothing for such and such other persons.]

In this blunt dismissal of a girl who may be facing the same problem as Henriette did, Charrière illustrates clearly the extent to which she has allied herself with her maid. By now, Henriette has become less of an abstract principle. Their alliance leads to the drawing up of battle lines when, as a result of Henriette's complaints concerning Rosette, the latter is barred from Charrière's room because it is "l'habitation l'asile le domicile d'Henriette" (4:50) [Henriette's habitation, asylum, domicile].

The end of the closeness characterizing the second stage of Charrière's relationship with Henriette and the beginning of the third stage will be marked in a letter to Benjamin Constant (26 August 1793) describing a quarrel with the maid: "J'eus bien du chagrin avant hier & hier. Il etoit du tant à ma bisarrerie qu'aux moins genereuses etrangetés d'Henriette" (4:159) [I was much pained the day before yesterday and yesterday. It was due as much to my oddity as to Henriette's more small-minded quirks]. Here the equality between them has been disrupted, as Henriette is more strange than Charrière. However, she then subsumes them both into the pronoun "on" in order to assess the significance of such a quarrel: "on apprend ses torts volontaires & involontaires" (4:159) [one learns of one's deliberate and unintended wrongs]. Such vacillation indicates the tension that has begun to surface in Charrière's perception of her maid.[23] This is signaled by the duplicity in which Charrière engages on the occasion of a visit from Constant. She cautions Constant to avoid indicating to Henriette that he knows about the quarrel (4:164). The agonizing tension between Charrière's solitary support of Henriette and the increasing weight of social and legal sanctions against the maid distinguishes the third stage. It is among these letters that we find both the most extreme declarations of Charrière's attachment to Henriette and the seeds of a rejection that will lead ultimately to casting out this problematic character.

The sanctions Henriette faced were exacerbated by a second illegitimate pregnancy, and the way in which Charrière announces this differs from her previous announcement about the first one. Writing to Constant, Charrière makes the consequences of this pregnancy, and not Henriette, her main point so that this second announcement of

Henriette's pregnancy differs greatly from the first one. She begins with mention of "un mariage fort triste que Henriette se vera forcée de faire si elle vit jusques là car je la trouve fort malade" [a very sad marriage that Henriette will find herself forced to accept, if she lives until then, for I find her very ill] and goes on to the resulting domestic rearrangements, namely M. de Charrière's decision to hire a servant of his own before the departure of Henriette (5:218–19). The consequences of the pregnancy tend to obscure the maid even though she is ill. During this period, Charrière engages in a legal correspondence to rectify the status of Henriette's illegitimate child. A letter written to the husband of Caroline de Sandoz-Rollin reveals just how peculiar Charrière's relationship to Henriette has become during this time. On 11 June 1795, Charrière writes him a note to congratulate him on the birth of a daughter and on his wife's safe recovery from the childbirth; four days later, she writes again, and this time there is more. Beginning with further commentary on Caroline's recovery, Charrière raises a matter that she had not broached in her first congratulatory missive. She reminds the husband that his newly delivered wife had been asked to find out the names of the members sitting on the committee that would hear the request concerning Henriette's illegitimate baby. Pointing out that it is Monday, she concludes: "Si dans la bagarre de l'accouchement ma sollicitation a été oubliée comme il est naturel, ecrivez s. v. p. aujourdhui" (5:107) [If in the brouhaha of the birth my request was forgotten, as is natural, please write today]. To prompt her friends in such a blunt manner to set aside their personal upheaval and attend to her request illustrates the tenacity with which Charrière acted on behalf of the ostracized Henriette.[24]

The social pressure on their relationship surfaces in extreme outbursts on the part of Charrière. On 29 November 1796, in a letter to a friend, she characterizes Henriette as "quelqu'un que ses fautes ont isolée, que mon support m'a achettée, qui n'a que moi au monde" [someone whose errors have isolated them, whom my support has bought me, who has only me in the world], asserting that "si on me l'ote je suis seule absolument" (5:268) [if she is taken away from me, I am absolutely alone]. One week later writing to another friend about the imbroglio into which Henriette has drawn her, Charrière does an about-turn and seems to wash her hands of the whole sordid mess: "Qu'on se tire d'affaire sans moi" (5:274) [Let them sort it out without me]. Shortly thereafter, Henriette is ordered into exile by the authorities and she leaves her mistress.

Whatever Henriette's experience during her exile was, Charrière suffered. Complaining of a servant's negligence in handing over a letter that had arrived the previous day, Charrière explodes in fury and grief:

De quoi ne depend-on pas! une servante met dans sa poche une lettre dont peut dependre le sort de plus que moi que mon repos & ma vie & c'est par hazard qu'elle la donne ou la garde! mon Dieu! cela ne m'arrivoit pas avec Henriette. Qu'on me la rende au nom du ciel! (5:293)

[Look at what we count on! A servant puts into her pocket a letter on which may depend the fate of more that me, of my peace, of my life, and it's by chance that she gives it to me or keeps it! My god! This never happened to me with Henriette. For god's sake, let them give her back to me!]

Charrière calms down once mail from Henriette starts arriving (5:299), and she is even unemotional when she records that Henriette might be going mad (5:302). The last stage has begun. In what reads like a farewell gesture, Charrière ponders the wonder of her relationship with Henriette, reflecting that she might have had a less tiring but more tedious maid (5:558). After this comment, Henriette is transformed from an unusual maid into an all too real human being.

The last stage of their relationship, the disengagement, involves Charrière's nephew, a young man to whom she wanted to be a mentor. Perhaps the role of mentor took priority over her role as defender of a woman pregnant out of wedlock. On 5 February 1800, her nephew writes that he would prefer his departure date be preset so that it would be clear that he was not leaving on account of Henriette (6:25), suggesting a certain timidity with regard to the maid. Two months later, writing to her nephew, Charrière makes an astonishing remark, noting that although Henriette had tried everything — pouting, crying, screaming, begging — it left her mistress unaffected (6:45). Charrière has now locked the unconventional Henriette into a conventional role: "Mon ton est doux quand elle ne sort pas des discours & des actions où je l'ai renfermée" [I speak kindly to her when she does not step out of the language and the behavior to which I have confined her]. Now the mistress treats the maid as society has, explaining that the maid must commit to the marriage that is under consideration: "Je serai bien aise de l'avoir laissé trouver une issue, un asyle honorable" (6:173) [It would put my mind at ease to have let her find a way out, an honorable asylum]. In this phrase, sending the maid away, echoes another phrase, one that had previously served to keep her nearby: the description of Charrière's room as Henriette's "habitation, asylum, domicile."

Charrière's sadness over the departure from her home of this woman, who had so embroiled her mistress in controversy, is soon ended. Charrière becomes uninterested, even in the idea that Henriette has made a bad marriage and is suffering (6:208). The penultimate reference to Henriette seals her in the identity of a woman who violated the social order. Writing to Constant, Charrière closes the book on this no longer extraordinary or even comprehensible individual. She notes that Henriette is married and that this has saved her: "Elle ne pouvoit aller de chez moi qu'au — mais un crane, il en est dans tous les états, m'en a debarassée" (215) [She could not leave us except to go to the — but a crackpot, there are some in every rank, has taken her off my hands]. The editors of the *Oeuvres complètes* assume, no doubt correctly, that the missing word is "bordello." Now on opposite sides, Charrière and Henriette are divided by the gulf separating good women from bad ones. In the transformation of the object "Henriette Monachon" as a function of Charrière's perception, the maid, from first embodying a principle dear to Charrière, went to being even closer to her in the second stage. In the vacillations and tensions characterizing the third stage of their relationship, the incompatibility between Henriette as seen through the eyes of Charrière ("my Henriette") and Henriette as seen through the ungenerous eyes of the neighbors affected Charrière's feelings for the ostracized girl. Finally, Charrière gave up on this personal *cause célèbre* and, rejecting her, saw in her only what others saw: a whore. In defending a woman pregnant out of wedlock, the author may not have experienced the condemnation that the pregnant woman did, but she certainly experienced isolation and a sense of disempowerment. For all her energy and devotion, Charrière's empathy and sympathy for Henriette was worn down by the force of social approbation when Henriette made it blatantly clear that she would not reform.

The Textual Self: "Zélide"

The following reading of Charrière through her self-portrait, "Zélide," is an effort to represent the female subject. This text is in two parts: the first, "Portrait de Mlle de Z ... sous le nom de Zélide," is one page: the second, "Addition au portrait de Zélide," is two pages. In the first part, a statement (the very first sentence, in fact) is made about her being good, and it will be the stated objective of the second part to work on this statement. However, the process of retouching the original portrait dominates. We will see that what has priority is not correcting the portrait but rather redefining what it does.

Portrait de Mlle de Z ... sous le nom de Zelide

> Compatissante par tempéremment, libérale et généreuse par penchant, Zélide n'est bonne que par principe; Quand elle est douce et facile, sachez lui en gré, c'est un effort. Quand elle est longtems civile et polie avec des gens dont elle ne se soucie pas, redoublez d'estime, c'est un martire. (10:37)

> [Empathetic by temperament, open-minded and generous by inclination, Zelide is good only as a matter of principle. When she is gentle and easy-going, be appreciative: it's an effort. When she is civil and polite for a long time with people for whom she does not care, have even more respect: she's a martyr.]

Addition au portrait de Zélide

> Vous le voulez donc, il faut revenir a Zélide. S'il ne s'agissoit que de faire un autre tableau, la chose seroit aisée. Ses amis disent qu'on en feroit vingt tous ressemblans a l'original, tous differens entre eux. Mais la tâche est plus difficile; il faut effacer quelques traits d'une ancienne ébauche, fruit négligé du désoeuvrement d'une soirée d'Autômne, et qui faite pour une seule amie, n'auroit jamais du être vue du public. On l'eut retouchée, si on avoit eu dessein de la répandre, a peine on la relue elle est echapée des mains. Bien des gens pensent, qu'on a fait tort a Zélide de dire qu'elle n'est *bonne que par principe*; Elle même appelle aujourd'hui d'un jugement qu'elle avoit approuvé: Si lon est bonne qu'and on pleure sur les malheureux, quand on met un prix infini au bonheur de tout être sensible, quand on sait se sacrifier aux autres, et qu'on ne sacrifie jamais les autres à soi, Zélide l'est naturellement, et le fut toujours, mais s'il suffit pour cela d'une scrupuleuse équité dans une âme généreuse compatissante et delicate, si pour être bonne, il faut encore dissimuler ses mécontentemens et ses dégouts, se taire qu'and on a raison respecter les foiblesses d'autrui, faire oublier a ceux qui ont des torts qu'ils nous affligent, Zélide souhaita toujours de l'être et le devient. (37–38; emphasis in the original)

[You want to. So we must return to Zelide. If it was only a matter of making another tableau, it would be easy. Her friends say that one could make twenty of them, all resembling the original, yet each dissimilar. But the task is more difficult. Some features of an old sketch, neglected offspring of an autumn evening, must be erased — a sketch which, made for a single girlfriend, should never have been seen by the public. One would have retouched it, if one had intended to pass it around; barely had it been reread, it slipped away. Many people believe that Zélide was misrepresented when it was said of her that she was *good only as a matter of principle*. Even she questions today a judgment that she once endorsed. If one is good when one cries for those who are unhappy, when one sets an infinite price on the happiness of every living being, when one knows how to sacrifice oneself for others and one never sacrifices others for oneself, then Zélide is naturally good and always was. But if to be good it suffices to possess scrupulous equity in a generous, empathetic, and delicate soul; if to be good one must also dissimulate one's discontent and one's distaste, stay silent when one is right, respect the weaknesses of others, make those who are in the wrong forget that they are paining us, Zélide always wanted to be this like this and is becoming so.]

The first description is static, the second one dynamic, setting up a distinction between on the one hand, what she is and was and, on the other hand, what she hopes to be and to become. In addition, by the terms of the first description, Zélide is good out of respect for an abstract principle; by the terms of the second one, she has, in the past, been naturally good and hopes, in the future, to become "unnaturally" good by learning to dissimulate. The tone in the first characterization of her goodness is dictatorial ("be appreciative ... have even more respect"). In the second one, the tone seems conciliatory; she will try to be a good girl. This, however, will prove to be a ruse.

At the beginning of the second portrait, what was written about Zélide's being good in the first one is described as that which must be erased. Note, however, that these are the words of a dissimulator-in-the-making. It is also true, according to the "Addition au portrait de Zélide," that the original statement concerning Zélide's good was contained in something not meant for "public," something that "slipped away." In this, we recognize the form of a secret, something that should have been kept private but was not. Coincidentally, the secret also happens to be the term to which an explicit and gendered value is assigned in this second portrait. In fact, the function of the secret in the "Addition" is to change not what Zélide is, good or not, but to place the burden of accuracy on those who perceive her.

The narrator states, "J'ai lu, que les hommes ne s'avent pas garder leur propre secret, ni les femmes le secret d'autrui" [I've read that men can't keep their own secret, nor women that of others]. The secret, then, is the criterion that serves to distinguish one gender from the other in this text. Applying this criterion to herself, the narrator asserts, "Mais en ceci, Zélide n'est point femme" [But in this, Zelide is not at all woman], suggesting that, like men, she does not keep her own secret. Here, we see she posits herself without qualification as not-woman. Significantly, in the first portrait, her gender had been given as a relative term: "Avec des organes moins sensibles, Zélide eut eu l'âme d'un grand homme, avec moins d'esprit et de raison, elle n'eut été qu'une femme foible" (37) [With less sensitive nerves, Zélide would have had the soul of a great man; with less wit and intelligence, she would have been only a weak woman]. At this point the retouching of the first portrait entails a change in gender and has the form of a secret. This change is effected in the giving out of one's secret.

Here is where the secret becomes truth, the portrait real. Although she would never give away someone else's secret, "le sien est a elle elle en dispose a sa fantaisie, ou plutôt Zélide na point de secret, que n'avoueroit-elle pas pour s'amuser et pour surprendre?" (39) [hers belongs to her, she disposes of it as she fancies, or rather Zélide has no secret; what wouldn't she confess in order to have fun and to startle people?]. In keeping nothing of herself secret, she literally gives herself away joyfully: "Elle se joue de ce qui la regarde seule" [She plays with what concerns only her]. In asserting the right of Zélide to this pleasure — the giving away of her secret — her portrait becomes real. There are two aspects to this. First, in giving away her secret she chooses to give priority to the present: "Lavenir est toujours sacrifié au présent, et ce présent devenu passé lui est encore cher" [The future is always sacrificed to the present. This present having become the past, it is still dear to her]. By annihilating the future, Zélide also annihilates the future of the dissimulating person ("Zélide always wanted to be like this and is becoming so") and preserves the person that she is naturally ("Zélide is naturally good and always was"). Secondly, by giving away her secret in this second portrait, she refuses to give in to people who cannot see: "Pour des vues malheureusement bornées, une légere tache obscurcit le plus beau tableau, pour de bons yeux le ridicule n'efface point l'éclat du mérite" (38) [For those whose vision is unhappily limited, a slight spot obscures the most handsome tableau. For those with good vision, the ridiculous in no way erases the glow of worthiness]. Her second portrait, in doing the work of retouching the first, changes the terms of the equation. No longer good or bad in and of herself, she is what she is regardless of the degree of accuracy the viewer/reader is qualified to bring to his perception of her. "Some features of an old sketch ... [are being] erased" and the original is becoming less perceptible (for some she may even be obscured by a slight spot) but also less vulnerable. At this point it would seem that Zélide has dissimulated: underneath the seemingly conciliatory tone of the "Addition" there lies a woman who refuses to apologize for what she is.

Zélide further refuses to give in to people who cannot read:

Si elle eut refléchi un instant, son portrait, ne courroit pas le monde, elle auroit bien senti, que la moitié des hommes sont méchans, et que cette moitié fait parler l'autre qui ne sait pas lire. Par bonheur le blâme de mille sots, et de dix mille prudes ne vaut pas un regret. Tous les jours Zélide est moins sensible au jugement d'une aveugle multitude. (39)

[If she had reflected a bit, her portrait would not be making the rounds; she would certainly have felt that half the world is mean and that this half makes talk the other half, who doesn't know how to read. Happily, the censure of a thousand fools and of ten thousand prudes is not worth regretting. Every day Zélide is less sensitive to the judgment of a blind multitude.]

Here, her increasing lack of vulnerability is made explicit. It is a far cry from the idea of trying to be good, of trying to satisfy the definitions others give of goodness when this does not suit one. In the relationship between the two portraits, a radical affirmation of her self is outlined, an affirmation that could not have been made by one portrait, or even the unproblematized idea of a portrait, alone.

The model for her portrait consisting of both parts is not a retouching, it is a taking pleasure in "what concerns only her," it is fulfillment in the freedom/control of the gesture of giving out her secret and becoming not-woman. While at first glance the second portrait seemed like an attempt to soften the aggressive tone of the first, giving the idea that she would try to become a good girl, in fact what we have here is a repetition of the aggressiveness embodied in the imperatives in the first portrait. The apparent softening or retraction, the effort to confine herself within limits, actually serves to sabotage the limits themselves.

Through the pleasure in "what concerns only her," the portrait of Zélide represents what is unique to the female subject. But this portrait also exceeded the identity woman, where woman is understood as that which must be contained within limits, the girl who must be good in a way that has been defined for her by social conventions. In this way, the portrait contests confining the female subject to an identity that can serve to disempower her. For a woman born more than two hundred years ago, the Zélide in Isabelle (Belle) Agneta (Agnès) Elisabeth van Tuyll van Serooskerken van Zuylen / Madame de Charrière is surprisingly modern.

Conclusion:
Getting a Word in Edgewise

Uniting the issues mentioned in chapters 4 and 5 — the meaning of woman's difference, the role that feminist biography can play — is the question, How can one speak for all women? Recognizing the physical characteristics women share must not obscure the important differences that singularize them.[1] Ongoing work by lesbian writers, for example, has highlighted the problem resulting from blindly assimilating heterosexual and homosexual women into one undifferentiated category. But a perception of woman as infinitely diversified according to various identifications (age, class, race, with or without children) deprives us of a political base and conceals what we do all have in common: a corporeal existence in a gendered society. Dismissing this corporeal existence as irrelevant is what Vicky Kirby rightly calls "a nonsense."[2] How, then, can one speak for all women? One of the most insightful models for such a standpoint comes from Linda Alcoff. Concerned by the limitations in either an essentialist or a poststructuralist definition of woman, she proposes "a positional definition" to avoid these limitations. To do so, Alcoff defines woman "relative to a constantly shifting context," which she compares to a chess board but whose parameters include economic, cultural, and ideological factors appropriate to the individual case.[3] Seen in this context, one woman can speak for all by speaking in a way that assigns priority to context and does not, therefore, imply the existence of woman as an absolute. To illustrate the form this could take in a literary text, which I will call getting a word in edgewise, I draw a paradigm from Charrière's *Asychis ou le Prince d'Egypte* (1798). This text is incomplete, and the editors of the *Oeuvres complètes* state that out of a possible twelve sections we have only parts of the first nine. Noting that it was written when Napoleon Bonaparte was beginning his Egyptian

adventure, and that it features explicit commentary on the duties of a
head of state, they classify *Asychis* in its conception as an allegory on
political power (9:361). No doubt this is what *Asychis* would be if we had
all twelve sections in their final form. The objective of my reading is not
to hypothesize about what is missing but to use this fragmented text as it
stands. *Asychis* can provide a paradigm for getting a word in edgewise, in
part precisely because it is fragmentary, meaning that there is no self-
contained or totalizable foundation. Equally important, *Asychis* is set in
an explicitly political context — a royal court — and is about speaking
— in this case, storytelling. These two aspects are not unrelated. The
court is described as the place where it is "presque aussi dangereux
d'écouter que de parler" (9:376) [almost as dangerous to listen as it is to
speak]. *Asychis*, then, links speaking with political action. In addition,
that it addresses the fate of a marginalized woman makes it a suitable text
from which to draw a paradigm for effective feminist discourse.

The plot concerns a foreign prince who travels to Memphis and
recounts his story to the neglected queen. In the fragment as it stands,
there are two other stories: one is told by another man, the other by a
woman. Isolating these three stories from the fragmentary text in order to
compare them makes the absence of other parts of *Asychis* less
significant. The three stories invite such a comparison because they share
a common focus on the problems that a father/father-king may pose, but
they reveal an important difference between what this means for a son
and what it means for a daughter. Considered in the order of their
appearance, they mark a progression: the three stories about father
trouble converge to set up the female storyteller's story as both the one
that is the most catastrophic and the one that integrates most inextricably
the personal and the political. Her story brings a different angle to what
father trouble means because she is a woman. Presenting the
subordination to which she is subject as a variation on that to which the
men are subject makes her experience significant with regard to her
difference from men, not with regard to her personal identity. The
paradigm I am proposing would be formed by convergence between the
three stories so that the woman's story is situated not in isolation (as
"Woman's story") but relative to the others. Differing from the previous
ones, the woman's story does not continue or amplify them; rather, it
interrupts the continuity with which a man's story is being repeated. In
this way it resembles what happens when one speaker manages to get a

word in edgewise during a conversation that is following a given direction. Reading Charrière's *Asychis* in this manner is meant to provide an example of a literary form that could articulate a commentary on the subordination of all women without positing woman as a homogeneous category. In the course of this reading I will highlight the women characters who are featured and the results of storytelling in each case.

The Son versus the Father

In the first story presented in *Asychis*, Lysandre loves a beautiful girl, Chariclée, but his father, who wants a wealthy daughter-in-law, has her kidnapped and sold into slavery. Following her trail, Lysandre arrives at the court in Memphis but cannot raise the money to buy her. His story features paternal opposition of a personal nature: his father is not a king, and he bases his objections on grounds other than political ones. The characterization of women in Lysandre's story is stereotypical. Even before she becomes a slave, Chariclée, being a dancing girl, represents woman as object. "La souplesse de sa taille, & la grace de ses mouvemens déciderent son état. On la voua à la profession de danseuse" (371) [The suppleness of her torso and the grace of her movements dictated her status. She was destined for the profession of dancing girl]. Bracketed between the significance of her body and the control of an omnipotent "on," the woman is figured in the sentence by nothing more that the feminine direct-object pronoun "la." The only other woman in this story is a girl who was induced to love Lysandre in an attempt to deter him from the dancing girl of whom his father disapproves. She is also object-like in that she is made to burn for him by another "on" rather than being in love with him on her own: "On l'enflamma pour moi" [She was made to desire me].

Lysandre toils as a gardener for Chariclée's owner while grieving over his inability to buy her, and one day he meets Asychis/"Iphile." Although a prince of Egypt, Asychis has come to Memphis in disguise and calls himself "Iphile." What prompts Lysandre to confide in Asychis is missing from the text, but in the part that we do have, Charrière lends importance to the act of storytelling by delaying it. First, Lysandre must interrogate the man of royal blood about his exact origins and his own feelings. Generous as he is, the prince is discomfited. "Asychis sourit avec une espèce d'embarras. Jamais encore il n'avoit été interrogé de la sorte, lui qui avoit mille fois interrogé les autres avec moins de discrétion" (370) [Asychis smiled, somewhat embarrassed. Never before had he been interrogated in this manner, he who had a thousand times interrogated others with less discretion]. In this case, the result of storytelling is male bonding embodied in the moment when Asychis holds Lysandre's dirty, sweaty hand despite the latter's embarrassment (371). The prince ends up feeling pleased and flattered that another has called upon him for assistance, and he vows to help Lysandre free the dancing girl/slave/woman he loves. While the results of this vow are not given in the text as it stands, Lysandre has at least acquired a prince for an ally. [4] The Lysandre story, then, centers on personal desire. It features woman as object and delineates a possible counter to paternal opposition in the form of a male ally. The next story presented in *Asychis* amplifies these two themes while introducing a political component, making the storyteller's situation more complex.

The Son/prince versus the Father/king

Lysandre tells his story to another man, but the next male storyteller, Asychis, will tell his story to a woman, the queen Aglaure. The legitimate wife of the king, Aglaure has been reduced to living in isolation at the court because she has failed to produce an heir. When Asychis shows up and seeks her out, she is surprised because no one else pays her any attention. They are blood relatives, however, and so he has come to confide in her after a particularly tumultuous period of his life. A great deal of the tension in the plot results from setting up the circumstances in which Asychis will tell his story, "ce qu'il ne devoit confier qu'à elle seule" (368) [what he must confide to her only]. Even more than in Lysandre's story, further details about the act of storytelling delay the act.[5] The queen agrees to respect Asychis's desire for secrecy and to call him "Iphile," but she is adamant about what this means with regard to her spouse, the king. Warning Asychis that he too must keep his secret, she dictates the rules governing his confiding in her.

> Il ne faudra pas [que le roi] l'apprenne jamais ... & si vous ne vous sentez pas la force de le taire toujours ne m'entretenez que comme vous feriez toute autre personne de la cour.... l'essentiel dit Aglaure, qui ne vouloit pas perdre

le plaisir d'entendre les récits du prince, l'essentiel est que le roi ignore que
j'en aie su plus que lui sur votre compte. (369)

["The king must never learn of this ... and if you do not feel that you have the
strength to suppress it always, do not speak to me except as you would to any
other person at court.... It is essential," said Aglaure, who did not wish to
lose the pleasure of hearing the tales of the prince. "It is essential that the
king not know that I knew more than he did about you."]

Aglaure deliberately sets up the prince's storytelling as a transgression,
so it comes as no surprise to learn later that the storytelling has initiated a
second transgression: the queen falls in love with Asychis, which puts
her in a vulnerable position. If it is essential that the king not know she
knew about Asychis, how much more dangerous would it be if he learned
of her illegitimate affections for the young prince? For his part, even if he
does not benefit, as Lysandre did, by telling his story, Asychis is not
harmed by having recounted it.

Turning now to the story, it melds Asychis's identity as son and as
incipient head of state into a whole and features two female characters
who, although extremely different from each other, represent equally
undesirable versions of woman. Significantly, Asychis never knew his
mother, as if he was born of his father alone, but he did know the sister
with whom he was raised: "Outre sa beauté & sa douceur qui étoit
extrême" (377) [Apart from her beauty and gentleness, which were
extreme], she was learned in both science and languages. In fact,
whatever Asychis knew of these subjects, she had taught him. The death
of this unconventional woman precipitates the upheaval in Asychis's life.
Upon her death, their father descends into obsessional grief, devoting
himself to the care of her mummy and neglecting affairs of state. In the
resulting void, ministers and courtiers try to tempt Asychis into usurping
power. These would-be revolutionaries are seconded by the woman who
has bewitched Asychis: Rhodope. She is as significant a female figure as
his sister in that, being defined by her specialty — "l'art de plaire & de
paroitre aimer" [the art of giving pleasure and of appearing to love] —
she represents quite obviously woman as prostitute (379). In this story,
then, the two female figures range from an intellectual to a prostitute.

Asychis is drawn into thinking about taking over, but before he can
act, his father surprises him with a birthday party. Later that night, the
prince observes the grotesque mummy of his sister being removed from

the palace for a decent burial. Was it the threat of Asychis's insurrection that, reaching his father, shook him from his obsession? No explanation is given, although it becomes known that his father was aware of this threat. The next day, Asychis and his father are reconciled and the description of this reconciliation charts Asychis's transformation: "J'avois recouvré un pere, je redevenois fils et sujet, mais je cessois d'être l'esclave d'une femme licencieuse, & le jouet de mes passions" (385) [I had recovered a father, I became once again son and subject, but I ceased being the slave of a licentious woman and the plaything of my passions]. After the abnormal situation in which the king privileged his dead daughter over the state, and the prince privileged a woman trained in "the art of giving pleasure," both men return to normal. While one woman was object, as in Lysandre's story, the other was an intellectual who had usurped the state in the king's mind. In any case, they must both be cast out for the men to recover their political identity. As the patriarch resumes his role of head of state, Asychis resumes his identity as son and political subject. This double identity represents an important difference from Lysandre, and it prefigures the next storyteller. An important similarity between Asychis and his father is set up when the two men recover their political identity by casting out the women to whom they had momentarily assigned too much importance.

In the progression from the first to the second storyteller, the sociopolitical status of the male is elevated. As in Lysandre's story, that of Asychis privileges male bonding, but of an even more powerful sort. The relationship between king and prince represents the continuity of the monarchy. Although the third storyteller, Zénobie, recounts more or less the same tale as Asychis, she is female, and the conclusion for her will be the opposite of what it was for him.

The Daughter/princess versus the Father/king

Although any details about the event of her storytelling are missing from the manuscript as it stands, on the very first page of *Asychis,* Zénobie is introduced as the daughter of a king who has lost his throne, in virtue of which she is treated "avec une negligence voisine du mépris" (365) [with a negligence bordering on disdain]. She tells her story to Aglaure and Asychis. Afterwards, Asychis, who was smitten from the moment her first saw her, is even more attracted to her. The details of their stories are remarkably similar: Zénobie's father, king of Thebes, lost not a daughter but his eyesight. His wife, who is an intellectual like the daughter in the previous story, tells him brusquely but with admirable logic that he should learn how to rule as a blind man. He turns his back on her, listening instead to charlatans and quacks who promise him a cure. At this point, Zénobie's story diverges from Asychis's. Sabacco, an aggressive neighbor probably modeled on Napoleon, sees an opportunity to acquire some more land and invades Thebes. In the resulting catastrophe, Zénobie, her mother, and her father each follow a different route. Before it is too late, Zénobie is sent to Memphis. Her mother commits suicide to avoid being raped by the invaders. Her father flees incognito and is never heard from again. While in the case of Asychis and his father's personal grief, political disaster was averted, in the case of Zénobie and her father's personal grief, it cannot be.

If *Asychis* were complete, the description of Sabacco's character (for whom there is no equivalent in Asychis's story) might account for this difference in the magnitude of the ensuing disaster. Working on the fragmentary text as fragmentary, one factor that emerges is the difference between what each father/king is mourning. Asychis's father mourns a loved one, Zénobie's father mourns an injury to his own body that makes him vulnerable. That it is the latter who is responsible for the greatest political catastrophe might imply that a physical injury does more damage to a king than a purely emotional one. However, the difference between what each father/king is mourning is minimized in a statement concerning Asychis's political philosophy. He admires Necus to the extent that this king "ne se livroit aveuglement à personne n'étoit l'esclave d'aucune femme ni d'aucun favori" (400) [entrusted himself blindly to no one and was the slave of neither woman nor courtier]. Within the context of Asychis, the choice of the adverb "blindly" cannot be innocent. Based on this declaration of what is admirable in a king, it would seem that the king who had lost his eyesight was no more injured than the king who had lost his daughter. Instead, they were both guilty of the same error: that of surrendering their autonomy. We should, then, look elsewhere to account for the different consequences that Asychis and Zénobie each experience when their father/king falls into despair. Setting Zénobie's story in the context of the Lysandre-Asychis-Zénobie progression provides such an explanation.

In the two previous stories, there were two female characters falling into the category of either object or out-of-her-place intellectual. Here we have only Zénobie's mother, who clearly belongs to the out-of-her-place intellectual, and Zénobie. What is she? Unlike the other female characters, Zénobie does not bear any misogynistic attributes, and she is the only one who becomes a storyteller. Nonetheless, she is completely disempowered, enduring "negligence that borders on disdain." Furthermore, the results she derives from her act of storytelling differ from those that the men derive. From storytelling, Lysandre acquires the advantages of male bonding, and Asychis enjoys confirmation of his newly recovered status as heir to the throne. In contrast, Zénobie's storytelling may provide the reader with an explanation of why she has come to be marginalized, but it has no results for the character. What, then, is this figure? She is a marker delineating the place of woman within a text where women bear misogynistic attributes and within a society where men bond with men in order to perpetuate the patriarchy. That the results of her storytelling do not affect her, but the reader, precludes reducing her to a woman speaking as a woman and thus does not imply any universal, transcendental feminine identity.

How can the fragments of this text, the three stories that are told, pertain to the problem of speaking about all women? In progressing from Lysandre, the son, to Asychis, the son-prince, and finally to Zénobie, the daughter-princess, the pertinent factor has been gender. The three plots concern father trouble and, because of the personal/political nature of the patriarch (father and leader), father trouble affects men and women differently. *Asychis* represents gender as an angle facilitating a politically significant questioning of society, illustrating a way for feminists to get a word in edgewise. Zénobie does not speak as woman but from the place of woman, so that the effect of juxtaposing the story of how woman is marginalized with the story how men are empowered interrupts the otherwise dominant account.

Heroines, Stereotypes, and Women

I do not want to end with the suggestion that this single fragmentary novel can provide us with a model for addressing a contemporary theoretical issue. Instead, I propose that all of Charrière's fiction in its diversity offers us fresh insights. What is consistently important in her work is the exposure of the diverse ways in which conformity to the socially prescribed meaning of gender may be enforced. From the implications of a heroine writing alone at her desk to the presupposition that an authoritative, objective, scientific voice is necessarily male — all these conventional and ultimately repressive stereotypes are excised with acuity through her novels. Treating the phenomenon of pregnancy, common to women, from varied perspectives outlines both an identity they have in common and an identity that in no way reduces them to being all the same. The vast range of issues appearing in her fiction illustrates the range of approaches that we should undertake in order to reveal the social significance of sexual difference.

Notes

Introduction

1.   Janet Whatley, "Isabelle de Charrière (1740–1805)," in *French Women Writers: A Bio-Bibliographical Source Book*, ed. Eva Martin Sartori and Dorothy Wynne Zimmerman (Westport, Conn.: Greenwood Press, 1991), 35–46.

2.   Isabelle de Charrière, *Oeuvres complètes,* ed. Jean-Daniel Candaux et al., 10 vols. (Amsterdam: G. A. van Oorschot, 1979–84), 3:92. Unless otherwise stated, the work of Isabelle de Charrière is quoted from this edition. References to the volume and page number of this work will be given parenthetically in the text.

3.   Elizabeth C. Goldsmith, "Authority, Authenticity, and the Publication of Letters by Women," in *Writing the Female Voice: Essays on Epistolary Literature*, ed. Elizabeth C. Goldsmith (Boston: Northeastern University Press, 1989), 48.

4.   Madelyn Gutwirth, *The Twilight of the Goddesses: Women and Representation in the French Revolutionary Era* (New Brunswick, N.J.: Rutgers University Press, 1992), 86. In his study of Madame de Graffigny's salon, English Showalter, Jr. explains that although the *salonnière* had to be mature, she also needed sex appeal and a younger sex object that she could make available: a "vivacious and vulnerable" woman who could "provid[e] a sort of complementary sexual interest." (English Showalter, Jr., "Madame de Graffigny and her Salon," *Studies in Eighteenth-Century Culture* 6 [1977]: 385.)

5.   In her discussion of Madame Tencin, Alice Parker offers a succinct formulation of the position occupied by educated women in the eighteenth century, stating that "there was no analogue in the political arena for the right of entry women had won for themselves in the social and literary spheres." (Alice Parker, "Madame de Tencin and the 'Mascarade' of Female Im/personation," *Eighteenth-Century Life* 9 [1985]: 67.)

6.   In Joan B. Landes's description of the gendered nature of revolutionary ideology, she underlines the schism that eventually characterized feminist rhetoric: "Feminist appeals to nature as the basis for equal rights for women ... were offset by claims about the natural grounds of sexual difference." (Joan B. Landes, *Women and the Public Sphere in the Age of the French Revolution* [Ithaca, N.Y.: Cornell University Press, 1988], 106.)

7.   Carole Pateman, *The Sexual Contract* (Cambridge, U. K.: Polity Press, 1988). Dorinda Outram, *The Body and the French Revolution: Sex, Class and Political Culture*

(New Haven: Yale University Press, 1989). Lynn Hunt, *The Family Romance of the French Revolution* (Berkeley: University of California Press, 1992).

8. Karen Offen, "The New Sexual Politics of French Revolutionary Historiography," *French Historical Studies* 16 (1990): 922.

9. One of the most astute overviews of this philosophical division is Susan Bordo's chapter on "Feminism, Postmodernism, and Gender Skepticism," in her *Unbearable Weight: Feminism, Western Culture, and the Body* (Berkeley: University of California Press, 1993). See also Linda Alcoff, "Cultural Feminism versus Post-structuralism: The Identity Crisis in Feminist Theory," *Signs* 13 (1988): 405–36, and Teresa de Lauretis, "Eccentric Subjects: Feminist Theory and Historical Consciousness," *Feminist Studies* 16, no. 1 (Spring 1990): 115–50. Additionally, Alice Jardine's *Gynesis: Configurations of Woman and Modernity* (Ithaca, N.Y.: Cornell University Press, 1985) remains one of the most thorough and exacting presentations of tensions in feminist theory.

10. Annette Kolodny, "Dancing through the Minefield; Some Observations on the Theory, Practice, and Politics of a Feminist Literary Criticism," in *The New Feminist Criticism: Essays on Women, Literature, and Theory*, ed. Elaine Showalter (New York: Pantheon Books, 1985), 162.

11. My study covers all the fiction in volumes 8 and 9 of Charrière's *Oeuvres complètes* with the following exceptions. Although a comparative analysis of works written in collaboration with a woman friend would be of great interest, I have excluded *Lettres d'Emilie à son père* (9:408–11) and *Louise et Albert, ou le danger d'être trop exigeant* (9:421–80) because they are not Charrière's exclusive work. Also I have not considered works published in languages other than French, namely *Briefweschsel zwischen des Herzogin von*** und der Fürstin von*** ihrer Tochter* (9:485–98), the pieces included in *Fragments de deux romans en anglais* (8:487–504), and the translation of Elizabeth Inchbald's *Nature and Art*, a novel published in 1796 (8:513–604). *Victoire, ou la vertu sans bruit* (9:504–6) is so fragmentary that even the title is only probable, a regrettable situation since it appears that Charrière may have had in mind a rewriting of the dilemma presented in Germaine de Staël's *Delphine* (9:501). Political allegories I discuss in an essay published elsewhere, so I have omitted from the present study *Aiglonette et Insinuante, ou la souplesse. Conte* (8:255–60), *L'Evasion du perroquet* (8:267), *De l'esprit et des rois. Trois Dialogues* (9:233–53), *Les Deux familles. Conte* (9:617–20), and *Lettres trouvées dans la neige* (10:226–54). Finally, I have also omitted, except for an occasional reference, manuscripts listed by the editors of the *Oeuvres complètes* as undatable; these are, in any case, largely fragmentary. The single exception to this principle is *Asychis ou le prince d'Egypte*, which I consider in my concluding chapter.

12. I use the term "heroine" rather than "female protagonist" here because I am referring to all that is implied by the term.

13. Pierre Fauchery, *La Destinée féminine dans le roman européen du dix-huitième siècle: 1713–1807. Essai de gynécomythie romanesque* (Paris: Armand Colin, 1972), and Nancy K. Miller, *The Heroine's Text: Readings in the French and English Novel, 1722–1782* (New York: Columbia University Press, 1980). Joan Hinde Stewart's *Gynographs: French Novels by Women of the late Eighteenth Century* (Lincoln: University of

Nebraska Press, 1993) is an important supplement and even corrective to our histories of the French novel. She is less concerned, however, with generalizing about the Enlightenment novel than are these other critics. Stewart's focus is on assessing the women authors she studies in their own specificity. It is only because of her different focus that I do not list her with May, Fauchery, and Miller. In the future, when the canon of eighteenth-century French literature has been revised and rewritten, there should no longer be a difference between a standard history and one that accounts for women writers. Joan DeJean's *Tender Geographies: Women and the Origins of the Novel in France* (New York: Columbia University Press, 1991) points to how such a history might be written.

14. Pateman, *The Sexual Contract*, 178.

15. Hélène Cixous, "Sorties: Out and Out: Attacks/Ways Out/Forays," in *The Feminist Reader: Essays in Gender and the Politics of Literary Criticism*, ed. Catherine Belsey and Jane Moore (New York: Basil Blackwell, 1989), 102.

Chapter 1
New Heroines: Countering Women's Fiction(s)

1. *Lettres portugaises, Lettres d'une péruvienne et d'autres romans d'amour par lettres*, ed. Bernard Bray and Isabelle Landy-Houillon (Paris: Flammarion, 1983).

2. In Isabelle Landy-Houillon's introduction to this novel, she cites the correspondence of Mme du Deffand and Horace Walpole and their use of it to threaten each other. (*Lettres portugaises*, 23.) Similarly, Linda Kauffman cites Mme de Sévigné's use of "une portugaise" to describe the type of letter that she will not write in response to an overly tender correspondent. (Linda S. Kauffman, *Discourses of Desire: Gender, Genre and Epistolary Fictions* [Ithaca, N.Y.: Cornell University Press, 1986], 95.) As an example of the force that a particular representation of woman can acquire, *Lettres portugaises* is perhaps overdetermined, but it denotes well the symbiotic relationship between social perceptions of women and the literary texts that both draw on and sustain them.

3. See, for example, Elizabeth L. Berg, "Iconoclastic Moments: Reading the *Sonnets for Helene*, Writing the *Portuguese Letters*," in *Poetics of Gender*, ed. Nancy K. Miller (New York: Columbia University Press, 1986), and Peggy Kamuf, "Writing like a Woman," in *Women and Language in Literature and Society*, ed. Sally McConnell-Ginet, Ruth Borker, and Nelly Furmen (New York: Praeger Publishers, 1980).

4. Nancy K. Miller, "Men's Reading, Women's Writing: Gender and the Rise of the Novel," in *Displacements: Women, Tradition, Literatures in French*, ed. Joan DeJean and Nancy K. Miller (Baltimore: The Johns Hopkins University Press, 1991), 41.

5. For example, images of women in both literature and art share a common ground in the eighteenth century. Thus, Gutwirth looks at revolutionary-era images of beautiful women drowning. With regard to paintings and novels, she emphasizes the force of these images which were so compelling because they "mirror[ed] men's desire." (Madelyn

Gutwirth, "The Engulfed Beloved: Representations of Dead and Dying Women in the Art and Literature of the Revolutionary Era," in *Rebel Daughters: Women and the French Revolution*, ed. Sara E. Melzer and Leslie W. Rabine [New York: Oxford University Press, 1992], 212.) My own concern is with less extreme images which nonetheless convey an equivalent force.

6.   *The Heroine's Text* is an early work by Miller. Her more recent essays on eighteenth-century woman-authored texts — for example, in *Subject to Change: Reading Feminist Writing* (New York: Columbia University Press, 1988) — draw on the methods of feminist literary criticism. Note Miller's qualification of the theoretical framework of *The Heroine's Text* in the version of "Men's Reading, Women's Writing: Gender and the Rise of the Novel" that was first printed in a special issue of *Yale French Studies* (75 [1988]: 47 n. 11). This note does not appear in the version of "Men's Reading" reprinted in 1991.

7.   Miller, *The Heroine's Text*, ix.

8.   Margaret Higonnet, "Speaking Silences: Women's Suicide," in *The Female Body in Western Culture: Contemporary Perspectives*, ed. Susan Rubin Suleiman (Cambridge, Mass.: Harvard University Press, 1985), 74.

9.   The insistence on presenting an archetypal heroine causes eighteenth-century novelists sometimes to stretch the limits of the believable, according to Vivienne Mylne. For example, she defines the dangerous boating trip in Jean-Jacques Rousseau's *Julie ou la Nouvelle Héloïse* which almost results in a shipwreck as "non-literal" because of the description he gives of Julie's actions during the crisis. Mylne asserts that Rousseau's "interest is concentrated on the notion of Julie as … fulfilling the universal rôle of Woman when her menfolk are in danger." (Vivienne Mylne, *The Eighteenth-Century French Novel: Techniques of Illusion* [Cambridge, Mass.: Cambridge University Press, 1981], 171.) Whatever the plot, the heroine's actions are dictated less by the particulars of their predicament and more by the stereotypes that both create and sustain such heroines.

10.   Fauchery, *La Destinée féminine*, 516, 653 (emphasis in the original; translation mine). Miller's review of this book is itself an excellent take on the problem of the heroine. (Nancy K. Miller, "The Exquisite Cadavers: Women in Eighteenth-Century Fiction," review of *La Destinée féminine*, by Pierre Fauchery, *Diacritics* 5 [1975]: 37– 43.)

11.   Fauchery classifies Charrière as one of those European women writers who represent woman's superiority in the form of their heroines' greater capacity for emotion and of their heros' inadequacy in this area. (*La Destinée féminine*, 581.) Thus, for him, the death of the loving but unloved Caliste in Charrière's *Lettres écrites de Lausanne* is ennobling (101). It is true that the male characters in Charrière's fiction often seem as if they are not quite able to cope with love. However, her female characters are more than just human beings endowed with extreme emotions; they function at several different levels. This is especially true of Caliste, a character who must be situated in the larger context of this two-part novel to be understood.

12.   Elizabeth J. MacArthur, "Devious Narratives: Refusal of Closure in Two Eighteenth-Century Epistolary Novels," *Eighteenth-Century Studies* 21, no. 1 (Fall 1987): 19 n. 29.

13. For a discussion of the epistolary form and its relationship to gender with particular regard to the image of woman, see Linda S. Kauffman, *Discourses of Desire: Gender, Genre and Epistolary Fictions* (Ithaca, N.Y.: Cornell University Press, 1986). For a telling example of this relationship, see Nancy K. Miller's analysis of a scene from a Jane Austen novel (*Persuasion*) in which it is not a woman but a man writing a love letter. Miller qualifies this scene, because of its allegorical value, as a "staging of the scene of reading, writing, and sexual difference." ("Rereading as a Woman: the Body in Practice," in *The Female Body in Western Culture: Contemporary Perspectives*, ed. Susan Rubin Suleiman [Cambridge, Mass.: Harvard University Press, 1985], 360.)

14. A figure such as Julie's brother, who laughs at her dilemma, appears to be a cardboard character. Although he boasts of how he has just cheated a fellow gambler, his crime appears not as a product of his personal vice but as a symptom of the degeneration of the aristocracy. Thus, Julie's reaction to his boast is to dream of escaping with Valaincourt so that she can go far away from representatives, like her brother, of what she ironically calls "cette aimable Noblesse" (32) [this worthy nobility].

15. La Fontaine, *Oeuvres complètes* (Paris: Editions du Seuil, 1965), 137. Translation mine.

16. Charrière makes a similar suggestion in an undated political parable, "Les deux familles" (9:617–20).

17. Fauchery, *La Destinée féminine*, 298.

18. We need to remember how unsuitable this marriage is. Michèle Mat-Hasquin comments on an even more unsuitable marriage in Charrière's play "L'Inconsolable" [The Unconsolable], a marriage that ties an aristocrat to a peasant girl. Mat-Hasquin emphasizes that the plot is organized so that this marriage is understood to have been authorized two years prior to the action shown on stage, as if to forestall criticism of such an outrageous match by virtue of its being a given within the fictional context presented. (Michèle Mat-Hasquin, "Dramaturgie et démistification dans les comédies d'Isabelle de Charrière," *Etudes sur le XVIIIe siècle* 8 [1981]: 63.)

19. Landes, *Women and the Public Sphere*, 46.

20. Denis Diderot, "Sur les femmes" [On women], in *Qu'est-ce qu'une femme?* [What is a woman?], ed. Elisabeth Badinter (Paris: P. O. L., 1989), 179. Translation mine.

21. Fauchery writes that the epistolary novel is founded on "attention à soi" [attention to oneself], but that this does not imply "clairvoyance." He suggests that part of the reader's pleasure depends on understanding the heroine better than she understands herself. (*La Destinée féminine*, 646 n. 6; translation mine.) From this point of view, the narrator's comment on Julie's dishonesty makes her even more disempowered, as it opposes the knowing narrator/reader to the unknowing heroine.

22. We know she has such portraits when she modestly remarks to Valaincourt, "Mes Grandes-meres ne sont pas belles, mais cela ne fait rien, elles sont anciennes" (25) [My grandmothers are not pretty, but that doesn't matter: they're ancient].

23. This is comparable to what happens in Françoise de Graffigny's *Lettres d'une péruvienne* (1747) when the kidnapped Zilia achieves financial independence as a result

of the stolen Peruvian gold throne that is melted down for her. In Julia Douthwaite's study of the novel, she describes this sacrilege with an exclamation: "The Peruvian icon, symbol of a patriarchal cult, is melted down and becomes the foundation for a woman's independent life!" (Julia Douthwaite, *Exotic Heroines: Literary Heroines and Cultural Strategies in Ancien Régime France* [Philadelphia: University of Pennsylvania Press, 1992], 124.) Julie's grandfatherly portraits are destroyed and not, one assumes, reworked (or even retrieved) to fulfill some new function. Furthermore, it was not Zilia herself who caused the gold to be melted down, whereas it is Julie who, on her own, destines the portraits for the murky moat. In this, the destruction of the portraits in Charrière's text seems a more aggressive gesture, although the end result, Julie's marriage to the man she loves, is less unconventional than Zilia's choice of an independent life.

24. Jean Starobinski, "Les *Lettres écrites de Lausanne* de Madame de Charrière: inhibition psychique et interdit social," in *Roman et lumières au XVIIIe siècle* (Paris: Editions Sociales, 1970), 147.

25. S. Dresden, "Madame de Charrière et le goût du témoin," *Neophilologus* 45 (1961): 266–67.

26. Julie's cry when, having crossed the moat by trampling on the graven images of her grandfathers, she finds that the door to the outside of the castle is locked, represents well this stepping outside the old structure: "Dieux! que deviendrai-je ... si je ne trouve point d'issue!" (33) [Heavens! What will I become ... if I can't find a way out!]. Indeed, it is as much a question of what she "will become" as it is a question of simply rejoining Valaincourt.

27. "Charrière, Isabelle-Agnès-Elisabeth van Tuyll van Serooskerken van Zuylen de (1740–1805)," in *Bloomsbury Guide to Women's Literature*, ed. Claire Buck (London: Bloomsbury, 1992), 410. *Lettres trouvées* was preceded by another text in a political vein, *Lettres trouvées dans la neige* [Letters found in the snow], also published in 1793 (10:226–54). The latter is more overtly political. Written in direct response to the unrest that the French Revolution had inspired in the area around Neuchâtel, it consists of commentary on social issues with no development of the two male characters who write to each other.

28. A letter she wrote in 1792 reveals just how unfeeling she must have seemed: "Depuis quelque tems je recommande l'étude de la logique à toutes les femmes que je rencontre. Les émigrées m'ont surtout persuadé qu'il faloit s'être accoutumé à raisonner avec une stricte justesse pour ne pas deraisonner grossierement dès que la douleur ou le desir, ou le ressentiment nous y invitent" (letter to Henriette L'Hardy, 5 April 1792; 3:352) [For some time now, I have been recommending the study of logic to all the women that I meet. The women émigrés especially have convinced me that one has to be accustomed to reasoning with strict exactitude in order not to miscalculate grossly once pain, desire, or resentment incite us to it].

29. In contrast to my interpretation, one of the editors of the *Oeuvres complètes* sees Pauline as unimportant. Jerome Vercruyesse's essay concerning the impact of the Revolution on Charrière's theater assimilates *Lettres trouvées* to her political writings. This means that for him the significance of Pauline is purely symbolic and does not make of *Lettres trouvées* a novel. (Jerome Vercruyesse, "Histoire et théâtre chez Isabelle de Charrière," *Revue d'histoire littéraire de la France* 85, no. 6 [1985]: 979–80.)

30. Pauline's mother had been afraid of being embarrassed: "Si on venoit à me reconnoitre malgré mon deguisement quelle risée! quel esclandre! Les railleries les plus insultantes feroient rougir ma respectable Mere & parviendroient jusqu'à Mon Mari" (480) [If I came to be recognized despite my disguise, what a big joke! What a brouhaha! The most insulting teasing would make my respectable mother blush and would reach even my husband].

31. Fonbrune met Pauline as a result of being wounded and then being housed in her castle. In a subsequent letter concerning his screaming nightmares, he once again addresses her in a letter to Alphonse: "Elle ... envoy[a] quelqu'un, qui ... demanda si c'était ma blessure qui me causait de si violentes douleurs ... C'est pis que cela, compâtissante Pauline; ce sont des spectres, ce sont de sanglans cadavres" (430) [She ... sent someone who ... asked if it was my wound that was causing me such violent pain ... It is worse than that, compassionate Pauline; it is specters, it is bloody cadavers].

32. Similarly, when she agrees to accept a ring from him, she formulates her acceptance as an imperative: "Oui, je le veux, donnez" (466) [Yes, I want it. Give it to me].

33. Stewart has described Charrière's use of the letter-novel as being "to describe the fleeting and the inconclusive," asserting that this genre "realizes its potential as the form best suited to writing the life of a woman and to exploring the unacknowledged control exercised by domestic concerns over female psychology." (Stewart, *Gynographs*, 97.) I agree, but I also find in Charrière's fiction evidence of an understanding of what may be implied by the affiliation between women and the letter-novel or letter writing itself.

34. In Isabelle Vissière's anthology of Charrière's works concerning the Revolution, she suggests that the author may have stopped here with *Lettres trouvées* because the magnitude of the changes taking place in the aftermath of 1789 made her hesitate to go too far with her own representation of these changes. Vissière describes *Lettres trouvées* as a little story written in the shadow of the Revolution. (*Isabelle de Charrière: Une aristocrate révolutionnaire. Ecrits 1788–1794* [Paris: Des Femmes, 1988], 368.) The focus of such an interpretation tends to obscure the evolution from one heroine to the next, and in no way accounts for the striking qualities of Pauline.

35. Douthwaite, *Exotic Heroines*, 13.

36. By gothic, I mean the literary genre first popularized in England by the success of Horace Walpole's *The Castle of Otranto* (1764). In George E. Haggerty's analysis of the gothic, he emphasizes that "from its first literary appearance [the term] implied not just a particular setting but a particular *use* of setting." (George E. Haggerty, *Gothic Fiction/Gothic Form* [University Park: The Pennsylvania State University Press, 1989], 11.) The description of the graveyard in *Sainte Anne* is clearly organized around such a use — namely, creating an emotional effect rather than conveying geographical details. In Alice M. Killen's study of the French reception of the gothic, she describes the origins of the genre by citing British poets who first began to "promener leurs lecteurs dans de noirs cimetières, hantés par les ombres de la mort" [walk their readers through black cemeteries haunted by the shadows of death]. (Alice M. Killen, *Le Roman terrifiant ou roman noir de Walpole à Anne Radcliffe et son influence sur la littérature française jusqu'en 1840* [Geneva: Slatkine Reprints, 1984], ix; translation mine.) Killen shows that the gothic

reached French literary circles later, long after its start in England, having become more appealing in Anne Radcliffe's work, giving 1797 as the significant date (77). In a letter Charrière wrote the following year, she reassured her correspondent about the collection of which *Sainte Anne* was a part: "Ne craignez ou n'esperez pas que ce soyent des ruines à Spectres ni même à Hiboux. Je ne donne pas dans le genre de Mrs Ratcliffe [sic]" (letter to Dudley Ryder, 5:443) [Do not fear or hope that there should be any ruins with specters or even with owls. I do not lean toward the Mrs. Ratcliffe genre]. The choice to include the graveyard scene in *Sainte Anne* must be understood not as giving into what was fashionable but as including, in a parodic manner, a genre she regarded as trivial. Later in 1802, Charrière writes to a friend that she regrets not having read a certain novel by Madame de Staël because "bon ou mauvais il m'auroit amusée. Elle y donnoit à ce qu'on m'a dit dans les spectres & les apparitions" (letter to Isabelle Morel-de Gélieu, 6:514) [good or bad it would have amused me. According to what I've heard, she leans toward specters and apparitions]. Charrière qualifies this style as "à la Ratcliffe" and then goes on to complain about the paucity of invention in contemporary literature.

37. In her interpretation of *Sainte Anne*, Whatley also emphasizes the development of a new type of reading. Her conclusion is supported by a consideration of a letter Charrière wrote to her nephew. According to Whatley, the author suggests through both her letter and her novel that "learning to read" represents learning how to negotiate a place for oneself within a society in transition. (Whatley, "Isabelle de Charrière," 42.)

38. The hyperbolic description of the resolution — "jamais on n'avoit montré tant d'amitié de générosité. Tonquedec étoit le meilleur des amis, Mademoiselle de Rhedon la plus généreuse des rivales" (9:306) [never had so much generosity, so much friendship been shown. Tonquedec was the best of friends, Miss Rhedon the most generous of rivals] — is similar to a description of a real situation Charrière described in a letter in 1762: "jamais on ne vit de parens plus delicats, d'amant plu honnête ni de fille plus irresolue" (letter to the Baron Constant d'Hermenches; 1:147) [never did one see parents more delicate, a lover more honest, nor a girl so irresolute].

39. Kamuf, "Writing like a Woman," 293.

40. In an undated fragment catalogued by the editors of the *Oeuvres complètes* as *Le Roman de Charles Cecil*, we find the following eloquent formulation: "N'est-il pas etrange, que le jugement même que l'on porte de la figure, que chacun voit, depende d'une opinion préalable, & qu'il faille à la plupart des gens l'autorité de la voix publique pour juger de ce qu'ils ont devant les yeux" (9:641–42) [Is it not strange that the judgment one passes on the person we all see depends on a preexisting opinion, and that most people need the authority of the public voice in order to judge what they have before their eyes]. Due to the uncertain status of the text, I do not treat it in the present study; however, it is hard to conceive of a statement that could describe so well the type of force exercised by *vraisemblance*.

41. Myra Jehlen, "Archimedes and the Paradox of Feminist Criticism," in *Feminisms: An Anthology of Literary Theory and Criticism*, ed. Robyn R. Warhol and Diane Price Herndl (New Brunswick, N.J.: Rutgers University Press, 1991), 95.

Chapter 2
The Doomed Heroine:
The Impasse of Revolutionary Ideology

1.   In Béatrice Didier's survey of Revolutionary-era literature, she points out that 1789 did not institute any type of "rupture" in literary production. (*La Littérature de la Révolution française* [Paris: Presses universitaires de France, 1988], 98.) She goes on to explain that for the most part, novels at this time did not address the political events directly, with the exception of novels concerning the emigration. The turmoil and bloodshed of the period was reflected in the "roman noir." See also Killen, *Le Roman terrifiant*, on the reception of the gothic novel in France at this time.

2.   Marie-Claire Vallois, "Exotic Femininity and the Rights of Man: *Paul et Virginie* and *Atala*, or the Revolution in Stasis," in *Rebel Daughters: Women and the French Revolution*, ed. Sara E. Melzer and Leslie W. Rabine (New York: Oxford University Press, 1992), 183.

3.   Pateman, *The Sexual Contract*, 112.

4.   A similar reading, oriented toward the representation of revolutionary ideology in fiction, is proposed with regard to Madame de Staël's *Corinne ou de l'Italie* by Doris Y. Kadish ("Narrating the French Revolution: the Example of Corinne," in *Germaine de Staël: Crossing the Borders*, ed. Madelyn Gutwirth, Avriel Goldberger, and Karyna Szmurlo (New Brunswick, N.J.: Rutgers University Press, 1991). Kadish emphasizes that Oswald, torn "between allegiance to the aristocratic patriarchal father and the bourgeois substitute father," assassinates both Corinne and the Republic (120).

5.   Vivienne Mylne points out, in commenting on Saint-Pierre's *Paul et Virginie*, that to have "the first-person narrator [be] a witness and a commentator rather than an actor, is not common in eighteenth-century fiction" (*The Eighteenth-Century French Novel,* 247).

6.   The first occurrence is to be found in a description of Henriette's visits to her aunt: "Pere Mere enfans domestiques combien nous l'aimions tous avec quel orgueil nous montrions au spectacle & aux promenades la plus leste la plus gentille la plus vive petite personne qui fut au monde" (294) [Father, mother, children, servants, how we all loved her. With what great pride we showed her off at the theater and along the promenade, the most graceful, the most kind, the most lively little person in the world].

7.   For example: "Apresent que notre heroïne est née" (293) [Now that our heroine has been born].

8.   Olympe de Gouges, "Déclaration des droits de la femme, dédiée à la reine" in *Olympe de Gouges: oeuvres* (Paris: Mercure de France, 1986), 107; translation mine. Even a critic who is not concentrating exclusively on women in the ancien régime points to the anger that came to be directed at women in a global manner: "The aristocratic body ... of pleasure and spectacle became the object of extremely violent attacks; in the process it received a gender: female. One figure dominated ... the worldly, aristocratic mother who forsook the duties of maternity and domesticity." (Roddey Reid, *Families in Jeopardy: Regulating the Social Body in France, 1750–1910* [Stanford, Calif.: Stanford

University Press, 1993]: 32–33.) This is an apt description of the tensions that will be embodied in the character of Madame de Valine.

9.   The essence of this loathsome image was distilled into the perception of Marie Antoinette, accused at her trial of incest with her eight-year-old son.

10.   See also page 291. In addition to these comments by the narrator, Sainte Anne himself accuses his mother of being more ambitious than maternal (281).

11.   This young man is presented as the embodiment of aristocratic foppishness: "Le jeune homme introduit par son Pere vint etaler toute son elegante nullité. Milton dit des tenebres de l'Enfer qu'elles etoient visibles et ici c'etoit une nullité visible, un vuide palpable" (315–16) [Introduced by his father, the young man came to display all his elegant nullity. Milton has said of the darkness of hell that it was a visible darkness. Here we had a visible nullity, a palpable void]. Of extremely ancient lineage herself, Charrière could nonetheless be incisive in her criticism of the aristocracy.

12.   "C'etoit chez son frere que se rassembloient tous ses amis ... c'etoit avec son frere qu'elle voyageoit ... c'etoit son frere qui donnoit toutes les fêtes brillantes" (406) [It was at her brother's home that all her friends gathered.... It was with her brother that she traveled.... It was her brother who threw all the splashy soirées].

13.   The father's choice of guardian is significant: "Pour comble de precaution il avoit attaché à son sort un des premiers amans de [Mme] de Valine homme d'esprit qu'elle avoit joué & ruiné" (406) [As the ultimate precaution, he had attached to his son's side one of the first lovers of Madame de Valine, a clever fellow that she had played with and ruined].

14.   Restif de la Bretonne's 1777 "Les Gynographes" (the title of which has been recently reappropriated by Stewart in her *Gynographs*) is exemplary in this regard. Bretonne cautions that raising women together is "prejudiciable à nos moeurs" (93) as it is conducive to "les communications corruptrices" between women and to a general loosening of moral standards. ("Les Gynographes," in *Oeuvres complètes*, vol. 3 [Paris: Edition du Trianon, 1931].) He warns that girls must be raised in a gentle manner, but "on évitera des baisers donnés et reçus" [one must avoid having kisses given and received].

15.   Henriette's description of the nightmarish scene with the two maids is presented in the context of her response to Richard's expression of desire for her. He says, "Je n'ai pas pretendu, je n'ai pas pensé ... mais je sens ..." (310) [I didn't aspire, I didn't think ... but I feel ...] and does not complete his sentence. Henriette does, confessing to Richard that she knows more than he knows: "J'ai pensé et pretendu pour Vous" [I thought and aspired for you], thereby indicating that her sexual desire for this unobtainable young man has been awakened.

16.   Outram, *The Body and the French Revolution*, 140.

17.   Gutwirth, *Twilight of the Goddesses*, 195.

18.   Elisabeth Badinter, in her study of the transformation that has taken place in the status of one and the other gender through the centuries, hit upon a particularly apt way of describing this. While noting that Jews and blacks were emancipated in 1791 and 1794, she comments that women were the "laissées-pour-compte de la Révolution." (*L'Un est l'autre: Des relations entre hommes et femmes* [Paris: Le Livre de Poche, 1986], 212.)

The expression refers to something that a customer orders but then leaves with the merchant because it seems substandard at the time of delivery.

19. Henri was confident he could leave his daughter in Paris (with the mob) and that she would behave. Concerning the behavior that he expects from her once she is no longer under his direct supervision, he writes: "Votre education rend superflues des instructions plus detaillées. ce n'est pas de lumieres que vous manquez & ce ne sera jamais sans le savoir que vous blesserez les moeurs ou votre pere" (356) [Your education makes superfluous any more detailed instructions. It is not reason that you lack, and it will never be unknowingly that you violate mores or your father]. We can see that his confidence is based on the assumption that she has internalized the ideal of virtue that was so repressive for women ("mores" or society precedes "your father").

20. "Je suis sans vraye & intime satisfaction" (388) [I lack any true or personal satisfaction].

21. "C'etoit Henriette qui fuyant le suplice du malheureux Favras arrivoit aux Echelles. Depuis le commencement de la révolution rien ne l'avoit indignée & ulcerée comme la sentence prononcée contre ce malheureux" (407 and 765 n. 18) [It was Henriette who, fleeing the torment of the unhappy Favras, was arriving at the Echelles castle. Since the beginning of the Revolution nothing had outraged and wounded her like the sentence handed down against this unhappy man].

22. The hypocrite who has been dominating Francoeur and pursuing Victorine is revealed for what he is when one of his letters is opened and read (404).

23. The topic they discuss is whether one should or should not openly express ideas about religion. In the novel, Honorine is tainted by the atheism expressed by the man who turns out to be her biological father. The effect is to make her feel lonely. She says to the man she loves, "Je regrette Dieu, Florentin, avec lui je n'étais pas si seule que je le suis à présent" (9:214) [I miss God, Florentin, with him I was not as alone as I am now]. When, later in the novel, Honorine displays a complete lack of apprehension at the thought of committing incest, her attitude does show the regrettable consequences of one man's having spoken freely of his religious opinions. In my reading of the novel, I am not pursuing the philosophical debate that Charrière explicitly addressed with *Honorine d'Userche*. This has been thoroughly studied by Alix Deguise's *Trois femmes: le monde de Madame de Charrière* (Geneva: Editions Slatkine, 1989). *Trois femmes* having been conceived by Charrière as a response to Immanuel Kant's categorical imperative, Deguise assesses the various ways in which the novelist responds to the philosopher. I am concerned instead with the way in which the novel, perhaps unintentionally, reflects aspects of revolutionary ideology pertinent to woman.

24. The parents' vain wish for a counterrevolution "les avoit empêché de vendre, lorsqu'il en étoit encore tems, un château en province et un hôtel qu'ils avoient à Paris" (9:43) [had stopped them from selling, while there was still time, a chateau in the countryside and a residence they had in Paris], suggesting that 1793 is the relevant year.

25. At another level, these two novels would seem to have been equivalent to each other in Charrière's mind since she considered using *Henriette et Richard* (written in 1792 but never published) to make a more substantial volume out of *Trois femmes*

(written in 1794/95) (8:277) before she proceeded to add *Honorine d'Userche* (probably composed in 1795/96) (9:171) instead.

    26.   It is difficult to conceive an elegant equivalent for the French neologism.

    27.   Hunt, *The Family Romance*, 36.

    28.   Pateman, *The Sexual Contract*, 77.

Chapter 3
The Last Word on Gendered Discourse: "To Be Continued"

    1.   Barbara Herrnstein Smith, "Value/Evaluation," in *Critical Terms for Literary Study*, ed. Frank Lentricchia and Thomas McLaughlin (Chicago: The University of Chicago Press, 1990), 184.

    2.   Genevieve Lloyd, *The Man of Reason: "Male" and "Female" in Western Philosophy* (Minneapolis: University of Minnesota Press, 1984).

    3.   Jacques Derrida gave an explanation of deconstruction in an early publication that serves as an apt description of this process: "It is a question of ... being alert to the implications, to the historical sedimentation of the language which we use." ("Structure, Sign, and Play in the Discourse of the Human Sciences," in *The Structuralist Controversy: The Languages of Criticism and the Sciences of Man*, ed. Richard Macksey and Eugenio Donato [Baltimore: The Johns Hopkins University Press], 271.) Derrida concludes that this endeavor is not "destruction," which is true of the type of analysis undertaken by Lloyd and of the reading of *Lettres écrites de Lausanne* and *Sir Walter Finch et son fils* proposed in this chapter.

    4.   With reference to these novels, Ronald Rosbottom suggests that "the general move away from first-person narration and toward the more 'neutral' third-person narrative voice in the early 19th century ... must have been a psychic relief to male writers who had been forced to 'write as women'" (Ronald C. Rosbottom, "The Novel and Gender Difference," in *A New History of French Literature*, ed. Denis Hollier [Cambridge, Mass.: Harvard University Press, 1989], 486), indicating the intensity of this link between gender and discourse.

    5.   These are two novels that Charrière thought about publishing together. In her last letter, a note to Benjamin Constant dictated to her husband on 10 December 1805, she proposed: "Peut-être imprimeroit on les Finch en même tems que Caliste" (6:611) [Perhaps the Finchs might be published at the same time as Caliste]. Charrière died in her sleep two weeks later. Had she published these two novels together, perhaps the most striking effect would have been to gather into one volume the two most outstanding examples of a character that tends to recur in her fiction: the passive male. In their relations with women, the unconsummated experiences of Sir Walter and his son are similar to those of Edouard and William in *Lettres écrites de Lausanne*. Jean Starobinski has suggested that *Lettres écrites de Lausanne* could be a veiled representation of male homosexuality ("Les *Lettres écrites de Lausanne* de Madame de Charrière"). The dizzying proliferation of exclusive male friendships in this later novel would then be a less veiled representation.

6.   DeJean, *Tender Geographies*, 50.

7.   One can only imagine what Charrière, who devoted a certain amount of energy to avoiding Mme de Staël's company, would have thought had she known that reference to this remark would become *de rigueur* in discussions of her conclusions.

8.   Because the issue of closure and the way in which it has been applied to this novel accounts for so much of what is written on Charrière in contemporary feminist criticism, I would like to summarize briefly the positions that have been taken. Critics of this novel may be divided into two groups: those who perceive points of comparison between the two parts and those who emphasize the division of the novel into disparate sections. The most representative of the first group is Susan K. Jackson; the title of her article, in fact, succinctly sums up the whole issue: "The Novels of Isabelle de Charrière, or, A Woman's Work is Never Done," *Studies in Eighteenth-Century Culture* 14 (1985): 299–306. She takes the position that *Lettres écrites de Lausanne* seems unfinished because Charrière chooses to plot feminine destiny as a paradigm. Implicitly setting up a contrast with the focus of conventional eighteenth-century novels, Jackson characterizes the focus in those of Charrière as the description of feminine destiny along the lines of women's handiwork: "Female life ... is rendered shapeless, open-ended ... but at least not necessarily or uniformly tragic, in close conformity with the model provided by female *ouvrage*." In contrast to most other critics, Jackson does not emphasize the finality of Caliste's fate, referring to it as "the infamous fatal moment ... displaced and disseminated throughout the life" (303). Like Jackson, Joan Hinde Stewart also judges that the theme of each part of *Lettres écrites de Lausanne* is embodied in what she terms the "indeterminacy" of each part. She concludes that this formal aspect "mimics the heroines' contingency, their social, economic, or affective estrangement." ("Designing Women" in *A New History of French Literature*, ed. Denis Hollier [Cambridge, Mass.: Harvard University Press, 1989], 556.) Finally, in his assessment of *Lettres écrites de Lausanne* in *Le Roman féminin*, Michel Mercier chooses to focus on the ressemblance at the level of plot, rather than at the formal level, between what he calls two apparently unconnected parts of this novel. He sees both Cécile and Caliste as representatives of women who do not oppose the social order that so arbitrarily excludes them. (*Le Roman Féminin* [Paris: Presses universitaires de France, 1976], 176.)

Instead of seeing a quality common to both parts, Jean Starobinski sees the relationship between the first and the second part as being one of degree. He defines the section featuring Caliste as the "version dramatisée" [dramatized version] of Cécile's life. ("Les *Lettres écrites de Lausanne* de Madame de Charrière," 133.) Monique Moser-Verrey elaborates on Starobinski's interpretation by pointing out that at the same time that Charrière wrote *Lettres écrites de Lausanne* she also wrote a play (*La Famille d'Ornac*) with the same plot structure (the problems of marrying off a young girl). The play, however, was resolved in a much more conventional way so that in light of this comparison, Cécile, although less complex than Caliste, is more complex than the young girl in the play. ("Isabelle de Charrière en quête d'une meilleure entente," *Stanford French Review* 11 [1987], 73.) Other critics have hypothesized that the sequel in *Lettres écrites de Lausanne* actually concludes the first part. This approach tends to emphasize the negative aspects of the sequel. In her book on Charrière's first three novels, Sigyn Minier-Birk treats *Lettres écrites de Lausanne* as a negative answer to the question, Will the young English lord ever marry Cécile? She considers the fate that befalls Caliste as a result of William's passivity to be a way of telling Cécile's mother that a man who is class conscious will never manage to overcome this barrier. (*Madame de Charrière: Les premiers romans* [Paris: Champion-Slatkine, 1987], 52.)

For two other critics, it is the conventional quality of the sequel that is pertinent, serving to abandon in some way the feminist interrogation sketched out in the first part. Elizabeth MacArthur views Caliste's life story, with its pathetic death-by-broken-heart ending for the heroine, not as an answer to Cécile's predicament but as camouflage for "the unconventional openness of Cécile's situation at the novel's end" (16). Her essay, "Devious Narratives: Refusal of Closure in Two Eighteenth-Century Novels," is a comparison of Charrière's novel with Graffigny's *Lettres d'une Péruvienne*, and MacArthur concludes that both authors had engaged in an audacious questioning of the way in which society marginalizes women. Charrière's questioning would have alienated readers of *Lettres écrites de Lausanne* except for the "compensation" represented by the more conventional sequel. Taking a more extreme position, Susan Lanser, in the most recent treatment of this two-part novel, sees the sequel as a way of selling out the feminist statement articulated by a female narrator in that first part. Lanser's *Fictions of Authority: Women Writers and Narrative Voice* (Ithaca, N.Y.: Cornell University Press, 1992) does not feature an entire chapter on *Lettres écrites de Lausanne*. Instead, she situates this novel relative to three other woman-authored novels in a discussion of the male Romantic voice that would soon dominate the literature of the early nineteenth century. Focusing on a moment at the beginning of the sequel where the death of an abandoned black servant is described, Lanser argues that this description represents the structure of the entire novel and accounts for the switch from a female to a male narrator. Although *Lettres écrites de Lausanne* "begins with the specific and political, it ends with the generic and metaphysical, 'Romanticating' a woman's material life" (161).

9.   Before publication of the *Oeuvres complètes* was finished, it would have been difficult for critics to consider these sequels without traveling to Europe. Nonetheless, Lanser does mention the existence of two sequels. (Lanser, "Courting Death: *Roman, romantisme,* and *Mistress Henley's* Narrative Practices," *Eighteenth-Century Life* 13 n.s. 1 [1989]: 59 n. 18.)

10.   Responding to Benjamin Constant's query concerning her giving up on yet another sequel, Charrière wrote: "Hélas! je n'ai point renoncé, mais où retrouver quelque enthousiasme, quelque persuasion que l'homme peut valoir quelque chose, que le mariage peut être un doux, tendre et fort lien, au lieu d'une raboteuse, pesante et pourtant fragile chaîne?" (3:231) [Alas, I have not given up on it, but where to find some enthusiasm, some conviction that man may be worth something, that marriage may be a gentle, tender, and strong bond instead of a cumbersome, weighty, and yet fragile chain?]. The letter is dated 30 August 1790, a moment when the bloody upheaval in France was far from ended.

11.   Goldsmith, "Authority, Authenticity," 48.

12.   Landes, *Women and the Public Sphere*, 53.

13.   Nancy K. Miller, "The Text's Heroine: A Feminist Critic and her Fictions," *Diacritics* 12 (1982): 51.

14.   "Si j'étois roi, je ne sais pas si je serois juste, quoique je voulusse l'être; mais voici assurément ce que je ferois" (142) [If I were king, I do not know if I would be just even though I should wish to be; but here definitely is what I would do].

15.   "Si vous aviez eu un ami qui perdant sa femme son enfant ou sa maitresse vous eut offert le spectacle que vous me donnez peut-être n'eussiez vous point perdu Caliste" (239) [If you had had a friend who, losing his wife, his child, or his mistress, had offered to you the spectacle that you offer me, perhaps you would not have lost Caliste].

16.   In her reading of *La Princesse de Clèves*, Peggy Kamuf proposes that because the princess is too strongly bonded to her mother, she can never find fulfillment in her sexual desire for Némours. The princess, in effect, disappears: "Ending as it began, the narration describes a sterile circle of the heroine's enclosure by the force of the mother's uninterrupted representation." (*Fictions of Feminine Desire: Disclosures of Heloise* [Lincoln: University of Nebraska Press, 1982], 97.) *Lettres écrites de Lausanne* assigns a different role to the mother because the mother's influence over the daughter is presented as temporary, as Sequel III makes clear.

17.   Her mother notes: "Il ne faut pourtant pas la trop montrer, de peur que les yeux ne se lassent; ni la trop divertir, de peur qu'elle ne puisse plus s'en passer, de peur aussi que ses tuteurs ne me grondent, de peur que les mères des autres ne disent, c'est bien mal entendu!" (138) [I must not show her off too much, in case people tire of looking; nor entertain her too much, in case she can no longer do without it, in case also that her tutors scold me, in case that the other girls' mothers say, Whatever can that woman be thinking!).

18.   His father foresaw this danger and feared that his son in the coming winter would become debauched without any real passion for it (243).

19.   In contrast to this close but not unbreakable mother-daughter relationship, we might consider the one in Saint-Pierre's *Paul et Virginie* where, as Naomi Schor asserts, "the intensity of the mother-daughter relationship results in a veritable taboo on the daughter's virginity." ("*Triste Amérique: Atala* and the Postrevolutionary Construction of Woman," in *Rebel Daughters: Women and the French Revolution*, ed. Sara E. Melzer and Leslie W. Rabine [New York: Oxford University Press, 1992], 148.) The sequels to Charrière's novel show that she did not envisage such a dead end for Cécile.

20.   In Janet Altman's study of epistolarity, she notes that "Letter narrative ... is charged with present-consciousness in both the temporal and the spatial sense. The letter writer is engaged in the impossible task of making present both events and addressee." (*Epistolarity: Approaches to a Form* [Columbus: Ohio State University Press, 1982], 187.) In fact, Cécile's letter differs from most letters in that it foregrounds this impossibility.

21.   Gutwirth also emphasizes the mother-daughter bond. She understands *Lettres écrites de Lausanne* as affirming that, in the absence of any hope for a fulfilling heterosexual relationship according to the norms dictated by society, a woman may find some "sweetness" in her relationship with a daughter by aiming for a "pared-down model of female aspiration, a subdued, but profound and kindly, maternal virtue." (*Twilight of the Goddesses*, 187.) This interpretation is based on a reading of the first part of the novel, which Gutwirth treats as an independent text.

22. Berg, "Iconclastic Moments," 220.

23. Douthwaite, *Exotic Heroines*, 126.

24. Cixous, "Sorties," 111.

25. Janet Altman, "Making Room for 'Peru': Graffigny's Novel Reconsidered," in *Dilemmes du roman: Essays in Honor of Georges May*, ed. Catharine Lafarge (Saratoga, Calif.: Anma Libri, 1989), 43.

26. Philip Stewart, *Imitation and Illusion in the French Memoir-Novel, 1700–1750* (New Haven: Yale University Press, 1969), 302.

27. Whatley, "Isabelle de Charrière," 42. Sir Walter describes himself in the following terms: "Je n'étois fait pour aucune charge publique. Dans le fonds je n'aime que les livres.... Je n'aime ni les expériences d'agriculture, ni aucune autre. Tantôt le bruit, tantôt l'odeur, tantôt la fatigue me rebute. En revanche, presque toutes les théories m'intéressent" (527) [I. was not made for any public position. At heart I like only books.... I don't like agricultural experiments or any other kind. On the other hand, almost all theories interest me].

28. Raymond Trousson's 1985 essay on Charrière and Rousseau remains an excellent overview of the connection between these two authors. (Raymond Trousson, "Isabelle de Charrière et Jean-Jacques Rousseau," *Bulletin de l'Académie Royale de Langue et Littératures Françaises* 43, no. 1 [1985]: 5–57.)

29. See also the very Rousseauist observations of children playing together on 544.

30. "Si je puis vous envoyer de tems en tems ce que j'aurai écrit je le ferai, si non vous le lirés à votre retour" (568) [If I can send to you from time to time what I will have written, I will do so. If not, you will read it upon your return].

31. "C'est une agréable réalité qui a pris la place d'un être auparavant fantastique" (569) [It is an agreable reality that has taken the place of a being heretofore a fantasy].

32. William refers to his father's encounter with the unknown woman as "cette rencontre qui a tant influé sur votre vie, qui influe tant sur tout mon sort" (569) [that encounter that so affected your life, that so affects my entire destiny].

33. If two women were breastfed as infants by the same wet-nurse, they are in a "soeur de lait" relationship.

34. In addition, William asks to be the godfather of the first child born to a couple he knows so that he and his own wet-nurse can be godparents together (588).

35. Barbara Johnson, "Teaching Ignorance: *L'Ecole des femmes*," *Yale French Studies* 63 (1982): 181–82.

Chapter 4
Interpreting Woman's Difference: Varieties of Pregnancies

1. Cixous, "Sorties," 113. Joyce Carol Oates, "Is There a Female Voice? Joyce Carol Oates Replies," *Women and Literature* 1 (1980): 11.

2. Drawing on controversial issues confronting women in America, Australia, and Britain, Carol Lee Bacchi qualifies the significance of this debate with the important proviso that particular, concrete political realities are of greater significance than this debate. For example, concerning the arguments about cases like baby 'M', she asks that "feminists involved in these debates bring the political conditions which have impelled them either to downplay or to eulogize motherhood onto the agenda, and not allow the debate to appear to be over women's sameness to or difference from men." (Carol Lee Bacchi, *Same Difference: Feminism and Sexual Difference* [Boston: Allen & Unwin, 1990], 201.) Certainly it is true that for any change affecting the status of women to have real value it must take into account regional, economic, and cultural factors. More generally, Bacchi's position reflects the division in feminism between the idea that changing the way people think can bring about an improvement in the lived experience of women and the idea that attention to theoretical issues detracts from practical and urgent problems that need solving on a case-by-case basis.

3. Catherine A. MacKinnon, *Toward a Feminist Theory of the State* (Cambridge, Mass.: Harvard University Press, 1989), 219–20.

4. Jean-Jacques Rousseau, *Emile, or on Education*, trans. Allan Bloom (New York: Basic Books, 1979), 361.

5. In a 1979 publication, Margaret Darrow advanced the idea that noblewomen deliberately accepted the new domesticity in an effort to "answer middle-class criticism of the nobility and, consequently, to forestall the political triumph of the bourgeoisie during the Restoration." ("French Noblewomen and the New Domesticity, 1750-1850," *Feminist Studies* 5, no. 1 [Spring/Summer 1979]: 41.) Her supporting documentation (first-person narratives of noblewomen) is at times ambiguous; it is difficult to tell if the women were deliberately changing or simply making do with the lot that had fallen to them.

6. Elisabeth Badinter, *L'Amour en plus; histoire de l'amour maternel (XVIIe–XXe siècle)* (Paris: Flammarion, 1980).

7. Kamuf points out that the use of the pronoun "us" can serve to "signa[l] a common and thus, in a sense, singular subject — or object — of feminist theory," a gesture that can betray a blindness to the complexities (even animosities, I would add) of current feminist thought. ("Replacing Feminist Criticism," *Diacritics* 12 [1982]: 43.) As I hope will be clear from my discussion, I am aware of these complexities and offer this reflection on the work of Charrière as a contribution to the dialogue, not as a party line.

8. MacKinnon, *Toward a Feminist Theory of the State*, 219.

9. Ibid., 220.

10. Margaret Homans, *Bearing the Word: Language and Female Experience in Nineteenth-Century Women's Writing* (Chicago: University of Chicago Press, 1986).

11. Susan Stanford Friedman, "Creativity and the Childbirth Metaphor: Gender Difference in Literary Discourse," in *Feminisms: an Anthology of Literary Theory and Criticism*, ed. Robyn R. Warhol and Diane Price Herndl (New Brunswick, N.J.: Rutgers University Press, 1991): 371–96.

12. Thomas Laqueur, *Making Sex: Body and Gender from the Greeks to Freud* (Cambridge, Mass.: Harvard University Press, 1990), 149–50.

13. Fauchery, *La Destinée féminine*, 402.

14. As Stewart notes, "Unlike many 18th-century novels, Charrière's major works contain no cases of mistaken identity or disfigurement by smallpox; nor a single duel, rape, purloined letter, secret marriage, or lost will." ("Designing Women," 554.)

15. Isabelle Brouard-Arens, *Vies et images maternelles dans la littérature française du dix-huitième siècle. Studies on Voltaire and the Eighteenth Century* 291 (Oxford: Voltaire Foundation, 1991), 339.

16. In the conclusion to *Le Mari sentimental*, the narration changes from first person to third person after M. Bompré writes, "Le remède est là; il m'attend. Adieu, mon cher ami.... Vivez heureux" [The remedy is there; it awaits me. Farewell, my dear friend.... Live happily]. (Samuel de Constant, *Le mari sentimental ou le mariage comme il y en a quelques-uns*, ed. Giovanni Riccioli [Milan: Cisalpino-Goliardica, 1975], 183; translation mine.) His death is then indicated by a loud noise that "répandit l'effroi dans la maison" [spread fear throughout the house]. M. Bompré's faithful servant also dies; Mrs. Bompré, however, "qui jouit des biens de son mari" [who enjoys her husband's wealth], remarries and lives a happy life with her hew spouse.

17. Some critics have blamed the tragic outcome of this marital mismatch on Mistress Henley. Thus, Minier-Birk, for example, condemns her for being frivolous, vain, proud, and egotistical. (*Madame de Charrière*, 40.) On the contrary, I tend to agree with Marie-Paule Laden, who views Mistriss Henley as an archetypal eighteenth-century heroine. Laden argues that the misfortunes that befall Mistriss Henley in her conjugal experience "aris[e] from the fact that [she] tries too hard and does too much, instead of being satisfied with the role of a passive spectator that society offers her." ("'Quel Aimable et cruel petit livre': Madame de Charrière's *Mistriss Henley*," *French Forum* 11, no. 3 (September 1986): 292.)

18. References are given parenthetically to the recent translation by Philip Stewart, which I use throughout my discussion. (Isabelle de Charrière, *Letters of Mistress Henley Published by her Friend*, trans. Philip Stewart and Jean Vache [New York: Modern Language Association, 1993].)

19. Laden, "'Quel Aimable,'" 296.

20. This belatedness is evident, for example, in the *Encyclopédie* article "Grossesse," which M. Goussier begins not with a definition but with a rather anxious discussion of how an anonymous (and very masculine) "on" can know if a woman is or is not pregnant. The answer is that only the movements of the fetus once they can be felt after the fourth month by placing one's hand on the woman's belly can guarantee pregnancy (958/260).

21. Oddly enough, Marianne herself omits any reference to her assumption of such an unusual role in her own letters.

22. Stewart emphasizes that this novel is set in a Calvinist society, where "pregnancy out of wedlock was punished with exile." (*Gynographs*, 130.)

23. Some critics have seen in Julianne a tart who did "tout son possible pour qu'une liaison s'amorce" [everything she could to strike up a liaison] between herself and the naive young fellow from out of town, as Minier-Birk puts it. (*Madame de Charrière*, 29; translation mine.) Other critics have read her as a sacrifice that makes Marianne's

potential happiness possible. Stewart has linked, in her reading of *Lettres neuchâteloises*, the fates that are outlined for Julianne and Marianne. She sees the result of young Henri Meyer's sexual adventure as "the pitting of one woman's fate against another's." (*Gynographs*, 121.)

24. There is no basis on which to anticipate that a woman in this position would, for example, be reduced to prostitution in order to support her baby, since she is relieved of responsibility for the child when she gives it up to Henri's uncle.

25. "An advance in intellectuality consists in deciding against direct sense-perception in favour of what are known as the higher intellectual processes.... It consists, for instance, in deciding that paternity is more important than maternity, although it cannot, like the latter, be established by the evidence of the senses." Freud goes on to assert that "men feel proud and exalted by every such advance." ("Moses and Monotheism," in *The Standard Edition of the Complete Psychological Works of Sigmund Freud*, trans. James Strachey [London: The Hogarth Press, 1986], vol. 23, pp. 117–18.) Indeed, they should, for, as E. Jane Burns has shown in her reading of representations of gender in Old French literature, the equivalence between "man dominat[ing] woman" and "the mind control[ling] the body" serves to conceal a very masculine anxiety: "Since man originates in woman biologically, her body provides the ultimate source for his privileged subjectivity." (*Bodytalk: When Women Speak in Old French Literature* [Philadelphia: University of Pennsylvania Press, 1993], 72.) Recent experiments aimed at making it possible for a man to carry a fetus in his belly may indicate the persistence of this anxiety.

26. Toril Moi, "Feminist, Female, Feminine," in *The Feminist Reader: Essays in Gender and the Politics of Literary Criticism*, ed. Catherine Belsey and Jane Moore (New York: Basil Blackwell, 1989), 117.

27. Nadine Bérenguier, "From Clarens to Hollow Park, Isabelle de Charrière's Quiet Revolution," *Studies in Eighteenth-Century Culture* 21 (1991): 235. See also Stewart, *Gynographs*, 203.

28. Luce Irigaray, *Sexes et parentés* (Paris: Editions de Minuit, 1987), 26.

29. Janet Altman, "The Politics of Epistolary Art," in *A New History of French Literature*, ed. Denis Hollier (Cambridge, Mass.: Harvard University Press, 1989), 420.

30. Pateman, *The Sexual Contract*, 36.

31. "Le problème est que, refusant à la mère son pouvoir d'engendrement, voulant être le seul créateur, le Père, selon notre culture, surimpose au monde charnel archaïque un univers de langue et de symboles qui ne s'y enracine plus, sinon comme ce qui fait trou dans le ventre des femmes et au lieu de leur identité" (Irigaray, *Sexes et parentés*, 28; translation mine).

32. Brouard-Arens makes the point that France was distinctive among European countries in that wet-nursing was more common than breastfeeding at this time. (Brouard-Arens, *Vies et images maternelles*, 44.)

33. Emilie and Constance had been in charge of clothing for the newborns, and out of a sense of egalitarianism they had made only one type of clothing.

34. Deguise, *Trois femmes: le monde,* 116.

35. In fact, this part of *Trois femmes* did not appear until the publication of Charrière's *Oeuvres complètes* in 1981.

36. "Comme ensorcelé il resta muet et immobile" (150) [As if bewitched, he remained mute and immobile].

37. "Bianca ... previt son malheur et pour n'etre pas temoin d'une infidelité qu'elle sentoit ne pouvoir supporter patiemment, elle supplia [Victor] de la renvoier ... à son ancienne Maitresse. Celui ci n'y vouloit pas consentir" (149) [Bianca ... foresaw her unhappy fate, and in order not to witness an infidelity she felt unable to tolerate patiently, she begged Victor to send her back ... to her previous mistress. He did not want to consent to this].

38. Unlike Bianca, the real-life Olympe de Gouges, author of the *Déclaration des droits de la femme et la citoyenne*, did plead pregnancy when facing the threat of execution. "While she maintained that equality, and not special privilege, was the only ground on which woman could stand, she nonetheless (unsuccessfully) sought special advantage by claiming that she was pregnant in order to avoid, or at least postpone, the death sentence conferred on her by the Jacobins in 1793." (Joan Wallach Scott, "'A Woman Who Has only Paradoxes to Offer:' Olympe de Gouges Claims Rights for Women," in *Rebel Daughters: Women and the French Revolution*, ed. Sara E. Melzer and Leslie W. Rabine [New York: Oxford University Press, 1992], 109.)

39. Homans, *Bearing the Word*, 29.

40. In the eighteenth century, as Lindsay Wilson has shown, the dispute over late births, and over who could validate or invalidate them, became the ground for an epistemological argument concerning the role of science in assessing woman's difference. (*Women and Medicine in the French Enlightenment; The Debate over 'Maladies des Femmes'* [Baltimore: The Johns Hopkins University Press, 1993], 162.) In asking who could decide if a late birth brought into this world a legitimate or an illegitimate infant, doctors, midwives, and philosophers alike entered uncharted territory over which women and scientists asserted their rights but for totally different reasons. It seems that we are no further from having resolved these questions than they were. Linda Alcoff asserts: "There are questions of importance to human beings that science alone cannot answer ... and yet these are questions that we can usefully address by combining scientific data with other logical, political, moral, pragmatic, and coherent considerations." ("Cultural Feminism," 429.) While I am suspicious of the term "logical" (it sounds like another version of "science alone"), I can only agree with her in light of the mirroring in our century of women's issues — namely, the status of their physical difference — that stimulated debate in the eighteenth century.

41. Irigaray, *Sexes et parentés*, 18.

42. Irigaray, "Comment devenir des femmes civiles?" in *Le Temps de la différence; pour une révolution pacifique* (Paris: Le Livre de Poche, 1989), 53–78.

Chapter 5
Belle/Agnès/Zélide/Madame de Charrière

1.   Liz Stanley, "Process in Feminist Biography and Feminist Epistemology," in *All Sides of the Subject: Women and Biography*, ed. Teresa Iles (New York: Teachers College Press, 1992), 11.

2.   In this, biography can serve a distinctly political function. Taking exceptional women to be "existential project[s]," Rachel Gutiérrez asks, "What better approach to understanding social injustice inflicted on women throughout the ages, than the biography of an exceptional woman, for to speak of a woman as exception because she did not fit into the stereotype is already to denounce the injustice of stereotypes." ("What Is a Feminist Biography?" in *All Sides of the Subject: Women and Biography*, ed. Teresa Iles [New York: Teachers College Press, 1992], 54.)

3.   Sharon O'Brien, "Feminist Theory and Literary Biography" in *Contesting the Subject: Essays in the Postmodern Theory and Practice of Biography and Biographical Criticism*, ed. William H. Epstein (West Lafayette, IN: Purdue University Press, 1991), 128.

4.   O'Brien, "Feminist Theory," 125.

5.   C. P. Courtney, *Isabelle de Charrière (Belle de Zuylen)* (Oxford: Voltaire Foundation, 1993) and Raymond Trousson, *Isabelle de Charrière, un destin de femme au XVIIIe siècle* (Paris: Hachette, 1994). Courtney's scholarly work runs just over 800 pages. It is both erudite and insightful. For example, in referring to the famous correspondence between Charrière and James Boswell, Courtney goes beyond a simplistic reading of their letters. "The odd thing is that they should take each other so literally: each accepts the persona of the other and confuses art with life" (117). Furthermore, Courtney is careful not to suppress Charrière's own voice. He cites her own letters extensively instead of summarizing them, opting to leave obscure some aspects of her life rather than jumping to conclusions about events that are not well documented. This biography was reviewed by Margaret Higonnet ("A French Jane Austen?" review of *Isabelle de Charrière* by C. P. Courtney, *Times Literary Supplement* 28 January 1994, pp. 12–13). As I have stated, it is not my intention to offer in the present study a biography in any way comparable to that of Courtney. We do cover similar ground, however, to the extent that we both discuss Henriette Monachon's role in the life of Charrière. Our interpretations of this role differ. Courtney assimilates Henriette to Charrière's home life, "a fixture in the Charrière household" (646), instead of focusing on what she might represent as a woman. Composed with a less scholarly audience in mind, Trousson's biography is shorter than the one by Courtney. Based on the premise that Francophone readers do not yet know Charrière properly, Trousson recounts in a lively, engaging manner Charrière's life both as an individual and an author. He compares her talent for observation to an entomologist's eye for minutiae (173), and in the summaries he offers of her novels emphasizes the way in which they grew from her observations of the world around her.

6.   Philippe Godet, *Madame de Charrière et ses amis d'après de nombreux documents inédits (1740–1805)* (Geneva: Slatkine Reprints, 1973), 2: 390; translation mine. Subsequent references and my translations will be given parenthetically in the text.

7. James Boswell figures among the suitors who were eventually rejected. See Irma Lustig, "Boswell and Zélide," *Isabelle de Charrière/Belle van Zuylen. Special issue of Eighteenth-Century Life* 13, no. 1 (1989): 10–15.

8. Isabelle de Charrière, *Four Tales by Zélide*, trans. Geoffrey Scott (New York: Charles Scribner's Sons, 1926), xii–xiii. Subsequent references will be given parenthetically in the text.

9. Simone de Beauvoir, *Le Deuxième sexe* (Paris: Gallimard, 1976), 2:318. The husband-strangling incident is glossed over in the English translation: "An odious husband may finally be murdered as the only way out of an intolerable situation." (Simone de Beauvoir, *The Second Sex*, trans. H. M. Parshley [New York: Vintage Books, 1989], 476.)

10. In Vissière's introduction to Charrière's political writings, she points out that because Scott saw himself in Benjamin Constant, he correspondingly saw in Charrière the older woman with whom Scott himself was involved. (*Isabelle de Charrière: Une aristocrate*, 9.)

11. Pierre Mahillon, "Isabelle de Charrière," *La Nouvelle Revue Française* 326 (March 1980): 105; translation mine.

12. Anthony West, *Mortal Wounds* (London: Robson, 1975), 215. Subsequent references will be given parenthetically in the text.

13. Isabelle Vissière, "Duo épistolaire ou duel idéologique? La correspondance de Madame de Charrière et de Benjamin Constant pendant la Révolution," in *Benjamin Constant et la Révolution Française* (Geneva: Droz, 1989), 33.

14. Translation mine. This sentence is omitted in the translation. (Beauvoir, *The Second Sex*, trans. H. M. Parshley, 477.)

15. Courtney discusses the possibility that Charrière was involved in an extramarital liaison in a chapter entitled, appropriately, "A Decade of Uncertainty (1776–1786)." He carefully debunks various hypotheses concerning the identity of the man she may have loved and hesitates to offer a truthful and detailed account about what will probably always be a "mystery" (*Isabelle de Charrière*, 339).

16. To illustrate how the multiplicity of a woman author's name can make it difficult to know this reality, Joan DeJean uses Charrière. Making the point that the first names of such authors are often lost underneath "madame" and "mademoiselle," she explains that "the consequences of this practice can be serious; for example, how many scholars working in the Bibliothèque Nationale would think to consult entries for both 'Charrière, Madame de' and 'Charrière, Isabelle'?" (DeJean, *Tender Geographies*, 2.)

17. O'Brien, "Feminist Theory," 130.

18. Susan K. Jackson, "Disengaging Isabelle: Professional Rhetoric and Female Friendship in the Correspondence of Mme de Charrière and Mlle de Gélieu," *Isabelle de Charrière/Belle van Zuylen. Speical issue of Eighteenth-Century Life* 13, no. 1 (1989): 28.

19. Vissière, *Isabelle de Charrière: Une aristocrate*, 11.

20. Jackson, "Disengaging Isabelle."

21.   Elizabeth J. MacArthur, *Extravagant Narratives: Closure and Dynamics in the Epistolary Form* (Princeton: Princeton University Press, 1990).

22.   See also 3:494 and 519.

23.   See also 4:469, 508, and 524–25.

24.   Henriette did not exactly reciprocate Charrière's commitment to her. Since she gave birth to her second child on 19 September 1796, she must have become pregnant in January of that year.

Conclusion: Getting a Word in Edgewise

1.   The necessity of also respecting physical characteristics that we do *not* share is emphasized in Ann Rosalind Jones's interrogation of the philosophy underlying *écriture féminine*. She asks, What can be the pertinence of *jouissance* to "African or Middle Eastern women who, as a result of pharaonic clitoridectomies, have neither lips nor clitoris through which to *jouir*?" ("Writing the Body: Toward an Understanding of l'*Ecriture féminine*," in *Feminist Criticism: Essays on Women, Literature, and Theory*, ed. Elaine Showalter [New York: Pantheon, 1985], 371.) At the other extreme, Bordo reasonably contests the tendency to deprive gender of any "material base" whatsoever, pointing out that, regardless of "the vast disparities in women's experiences of childbirth" it nonetheless gives them more in common with each other than with men. (*Unbearable Weight*, 230.) The different points these critics make illustrate the complexity of trying to theorize the fact of woman's body.

2.   Vicky Kirby, "Corporeal Habits: Addressing Essentialism Differently," *Hypatia* 6 (1991): 17.

3.   Linda Alcoff, "Cultural Feminism," 433. Her model has the further advantage of facilitating political action because it allows feminist claims for greater social justice to be formulated as claims that "their position within the network lacks power and mobility and requires radical change" (434).

4.   It seems that Asychis will be a strong ally, for he thinks in these terms: "Non seulement il avoit un ami mais il étoit un ami" (373) [He not only had a friend, he was a friend].

5.   The tent that Aglaure will set up for their conversations must be described, and the reason for which they must break off if any interloper appears must be explained. In the end, it will take two days for Asychis to tell his story to the neglected queen at the court of Necus.

Bibliography

Works by Isabelle de Charrière

Charrière, Isabelle de. *Caliste ou Lettres écrites de Lausanne*. Preface by Claudine Herrmann. Paris: Des Femmes, 1971.

———. *Four Tales by Zélide*. Translated by Geoffrey Scott. New York: Charles Scribner's Sons, 1926.

———. *Isabelle de Charrière: Une aristocrate révolutionnaire. Ecrits 1788–1794*. Edited by Isabelle Vissière. Paris: Des Femmes, 1988.

———. *Letters of Mistress Henley Published by Her Friend*. Translated by Philip Stewart and Jean Vache. New York: Modern Language Association, 1993.

———. *Lettres de Mistriss Henley publiées par son amie*. Edited by Joan Hinde Stewart and Philip Stewart. New York: Modern Language Association, 1993.

———. *Une Liaison dangereuse; une correspondance avec Constant d'Hermenches 1760–1776*. Edited by Isabelle and Jean-Louis Vissière. Paris: La Différence, 1991.

———. *Oeuvres complètes*. Edited by Jean-Daniel Candaux, C. P. Courtney, Pierre H. Dubois, Simone Dubois-De Bruyn, Patrice Thompson, Jeroom Vercruysse, and Dennis M. Wood. 10 vols. Amsterdam: G. A. van Oorschot, 1979–84.

———. *Romans: Lettres écrites de Lausanne, Trois femmes, Lettres de Mistriss Henley, Lettres neuchâteloises*. Paris: Chemin Vert, 1982.

Other Works Cited

Alcoff, Linda. "Cultural Feminism versus Post-structuralism: The Identity Crisis in Feminist Theory." *Signs* 13 (1988): 405–36.

Altman, Janet Gurkin. *Epistolarity: Approaches to a Form*. Columbus: Ohio State University Press, 1982.

———. "Making Room for 'Peru': Graffigny's Novel Reconsidered." In *Dilemmes du roman: Essays in Honor of Georges May*, edited by Catharine Lafarge, 33–46. Saratoga, Calif.: Anma Libri, 1989.

———. "The Politics of Epistolary Art." In *A New History of French Literature,* edited by Denis Hollier, 415–21. Cambridge, Mass.: Harvard University Press, 1989.

Bacchi, Carol Lee. *Same Difference: Feminism and Sexual Difference*. Boston: Allen & Unwin, 1990.

Badinter, Elisabeth. *L'Amour en plus; histoire de l'amour maternel (XVIIe-XXe siècle)*. Paris: Flammarion, 1980.

———. *L'Un est l'autre: Des relations entre hommes et femmes*. Paris: Le Livre de Poche, 1986.

Beauvoir, Simone de. *Le Deuxième sexe*. 2 vols. Paris: Gallimard, 1976.

———. *The Second Sex*. Translated by H. M. Parshley. New York: Vintage Books, 1989.

Bérenguier, Nadine. "From Clarens to Hollow Park, Isabelle de Charrière's Quiet Revolution." *Studies in Eighteenth-Century Culture* 21 (1991): 219–42.

Berg, Elizabeth L. "Iconoclastic Moments: Reading the *Sonnets for Helene*, Writing the *Portuguese Letters*." In *Poetics of Gender,* edited by Nancy K. Miller, 208–21. New York: Columbia University Press, 1986.

Bordo, Susan. *Unbearable Weight: Feminism, Western Culture, and the Body*. Berkeley and Los Angeles: University of California Press, 1993.

Bretonne, Restif de la. "Les Gynographes." In *Oeuvres complètes,* vol. 3, pp. 91–130. Paris: Edition du Trianon, 1931.

Brouard-Arens, Isabelle. *Vies et images maternelles dans la littérature française du dix-huitième siècle. Studies on Voltaire and the Eighteenth Century* 291. Oxford: Voltaire Foundation, 1991.

Burns, E. Jane. *Bodytalk: When Women Speak in Old French Literature*. Philadelphia: University of Pennsylvania Press, 1993.

"Charrière, Isabelle-Agnès-Elisabeth van Tuyll van Serooskerken van Zuylen de (1740–1805)." In *Bloomsbury Guide to Women's Literature*, edited by Claire Buck. London: Bloomsbury, 1992.

Cixous, Hélène. "Sorties: Out and Out: Attacks/Ways Out/Forays." In *The Feminist Reader: Essays in Gender and the Politics of Literary*

Criticism, edited by Catherine Belsey and Jane Moore, 101–16. New York: Basil Blackwell, 1989.

Constant, Samuel de. *Le mari sentimental ou le mariage comme il y en a quelques-uns*. Edited by Giovanni Riccioli. Milan: Cisalpino-Goliardica, 1975.

Courtney, C. P. *Isabelle de Charrière (Belle de Zuylen). A Biography*. Oxford: Voltaire Foundation, Taylor Institution, 1993,

Darrow, Margaret H. "French Noblewomen and the New Domesticity, 1750–1850." *Feminist Studies* 5, no. 1 (Spring 1979): 41–65.

Deguise, Alix. *Trois femmes: le monde de Madame de Charrière*. Geneva: Editions Slatkine, 1989.

DeJean, Joan. *Tender Geographies: Women and the Origins of the Novel in France*. New York: Columbia University Press, 1991.

Derrida, Jacques. "Structure, Sign, and Play in the Discourse of the Human Sciences." In *The Structuralist Controversy: The Languages of Criticism and the Sciences of Man*, edited by Richard Macksey and Eugenio Donato, 247–72. Baltimore: The Johns Hopkins University Press, 1972.

Diderot, Denis. "Sur les femmes." In *Qu'est qu'une femme?* edited and with preface by Elisabeth Badinter, 163–85. Paris: P. O. L., 1989.

Didier, Béatrice. *La Littérature de la Révolution française*. Paris: Presses universitaires de France, 1988.

Douthwaite, Julia V. *Exotic Heroines: Literary Heroines and Cultural Strategies in Ancien Régime France*. Philadelphia: University of Pennsylvania Press, 1992.

Dresden, S. "Mme de Charrière et le goût du témoin." *Neophilologus* 45 (1961): 261–78.

Fauchery, Pierre. *La Destinée féminine dans le roman européen du dix-huitième siècle: 1713–1807. Essai de gynécomythie romanesque*. Paris: Armand Colin, 1972.

Freud, Sigmund. "Moses and Monotheism." In *The Standard Edition of the Complete Psychological Works of Sigmund Freud*, translated by James Strachey, vol. 23. London: The Hogarth Press, 1964.

Friedman, Susan Stanford. "Creativity and the Childbirth Metaphor: Gender Difference in Literary Discourse." In *Feminisms: an Anthology of Literary Theory and Criticism*, edited by Robyn R. Warhol and Diane Price Herndl, 371–96. New Brunswick, N. J.: Rutgers University Press, 1991.

Godet, Philippe. *Madame de Charrière et ses amis d'après de nombreux documents inédits (1740–1805)*. Geneva: Slatkine Reprints, 1973.

Goldsmith, Elizabeth C. "Authority, Authenticity, and the Publication of Letters by Women." In *Writing the Female Voice: Essays on Epistolary Literature,* edited by Elizabeth C. Goldsmith, 46–59. Boston: Northeastern University Press, 1989.

Gouges, Olympe de. "Déclaration des droits de la femme dédiée à la reine." In *Olympe de Gouges: oeuvres,* 99–112. Paris: Mercure de France, 1986.

Gutiérrez, Rachel. "What Is a Feminist Biography?" In *All Sides of the Subject: Women and Biography,* edited by Teresa Iles, 48–55. New York: Teachers College Press, 1992.

Gutwirth, Madelyn. "The Engulfed Beloved: Representations of Dead and Dying Women in the Art and Literature of the Revolutionary Era." In *Rebel Daughters: Women and the French Revolution,* edited by Sara E. Melzer and Leslie W. Rabine, 198–227. New York: Oxford University Press, 1992.

———. *The Twilight of the Goddesses: Women and Representation in the French Revolutionary Era*. New Brunswick, N. J.: Rutgers University Press, 1992.

Haggerty, George E. *Gothic Fiction/Gothic Form*. University Park, PA: The Pennsylvania State University Press, 1989.

Higonnet, Margaret. "A French Jane Austen?" Review of *Isabelle de Charrière*, by C. P. Courtney. *Times Literary Supplement* 28 January 1994, pp. 12–13.

———. "Speaking Silences: Women's Suicide." In *The Female Body in Western Culture: Contemporary Perspectives,* edited by Susan Rubin Suleiman, 68–83. Cambridge, Mass.: Harvard University Press, 1985.

Homans, Margaret. *Bearing the Word: Language and Female Experience in Nineteenth-Century Women's Writing*. Chicago: University of Chicago Press, 1986.

Hunt, Lynn. *The Family Romance of the French Revolution*. Berkeley: University of California Press, 1992.

Irigaray, Luce. *Sexes et parentés*. Paris: Editions de Minuit, 1987.

———. *Le Temps de la différence; pour une révolution pacifique*. Paris: Le Livre de Poche, 1989.

Jackson, Susan K. "Disengaging Isabelle: Professional Rhetoric and Female Friendship in the Correspondence of Mme de Charrière and

Mlle de Gélieu." *Eighteenth-Century Life* 13, n.s. 1 (1989): 26–41. Special issue: "Isabelle de Charrière: Belle Van Zuylen." Edited by Beatrice Fink..

———. "The Novels of Isabelle de Charrière, or, A Woman's Work Is Never Done." *Studies in Eighteenth-Century Culture* 14 (1985): 299–306.

Jardine, Alice. *Gynesis: Configurations of Woman and Modernity.* Ithaca, N. Y.: Cornell University Press, 1985.

Jehlen, Myra. "Archimedes and the Paradox of Feminist Criticism." In *Feminisms: An Anthology of Literary Theory and Criticism,* edited by Robyn R. Warhol and Diane Price Herndl, 75–96. New Brunswick, N. J.: Rutgers University Press, 1991.

Johnson, Barbara. "Teaching Ignorance: *L'Ecole des femmes.*" *Yale French Studies* 63 (1982): 165–82.

Jones, Ann Rosalind. "Writing the Body: Toward an Understanding of l' *Ecriture féminine.*" In *The New Feminist Criticism,* edited by Elaine Showalter, 361–77. New York: Pantheon, 1985.

Kadish, Doris Y. "Narrating the French Revolution: the Example of *Corinne.*" In *Germaine de Staël: Crossing the Borders,* edited by Madelyn Gutwirth, Avriel Goldberger, and Karyna Szmurlo, 113–21. New Brunswick, N. J.: Rutgers University Press, 1991.

Kamuf, Peggy. *Fictions of Feminine Desire: Disclosures of Heloise.* Lincoln: University of Nebraska Press, 1982.

———. "Replacing Feminist Criticism." *Diacritics* 12 (1982): 42–47.

———. "Writing like a Woman." In *Women and Language in Literature and Society,* edited by Sally McConnell-Ginet, Ruth Borker, and Nelly Furmen, 284–300. New York: Praeger Publishers, 1980.

Kauffmann, Linda S. *Discourses of Desire: Gender, Genre and Epistolary Fictions.* Ithaca, N. Y.: Cornell University Press, 1986.

Killen, Alice M. *Le Roman terrifiant ou roman noir de Walpole à Anne Radcliffe et son influence sur la littérature française jusqu'en 1840.* 1967. Reprint, Geneva: Slatkine Reprints, 1984.

Kirby, Vicki. "Corporeal Habits: Addressing Essentialism Differently." *Hypatia* 6 (1991): 4–24.

Kolodny, Annette. "Dancing through the Minefield; Some Observations on the Theory, Practice, and Politics of a Feminist Literary Criticism." In *The New Feminist Criticism; Essays on Women, Literature, and*

Theory, edited by Elaine Showalter, 144–67. New York: Pantheon Books, 1985.

La Fontaine. *Oeuvres complètes.* Paris: Editions du Seuil, 1965.

Laden, Marie-Paule. "'Quel aimable et cruel petit livre': Madame de Charrière's *Mistriss Henley.*" *French Forum* 11, no. 3 (September 1986): 289–99.

Landes, Joan B. *Women and the Public Sphere in the Age of the French Revolution.* Ithaca, N. Y.: Cornell University Press, 1988.

Lanser, Susan S. *Fictions of Authority: Women Writers and Narrative Voice.* Ithaca, N. Y.: Cornell University Press, 1992.

———. "Courting Death: Roman, romantisme, and Mistress Henley's Narrative Practices." In *Eighteenth-Century Life* 13, n.s. 1 (1989): 49. Special issue: "Isabelle de Charrière: Belle Van Zuylen." Edited by Beatrice Fink.

Laqueur, Thomas. *Making Sex: Body and Gender from the Greeks to Freud.* Cambridge, Mass.: Harvard University Press, 1990.

Lauretis, Teresa de. "Eccentric Subjects: Feminist Theory and Historical Consciousness." *Feminist Studies* 16, no. 1 (Spring 1990): 115–50.

Lettres portugaises, Lettres d'une Péruvienne et d'autres romans d'amour par lettres. Edited by Bernard Bray and Isabelle Landy-Houillon. Introduction by Isabelle Landy-Houillon. Paris: Flammarion, 1983.

Lloyd, Genevieve. *The Man of Reason: "Male" and "Female" in Western Philosophy.* Minneapolis: University of Minnesota Press, 1984.

Lustig, Irma. "Boswell and Zélide." In *Eighteenth-Century Life* 13, n.s. 1 (1989): 10–15. Special issue: "Isabelle de Charrière: Belle Van Zuylen." Edited by Beatrice Fink.

MacArthur, Elizabeth J. "Devious Narratives: Refusal of Closure in Two Eighteenth-Century Epistolary Novels." *Eighteenth-Century Studies* 21, no. 1 (Fall 1987): 1–20.

———. *Extravagant Narratives: Closure and Dynamics in the Epistolary Form.* Princeton, N. J.: Princeton University Press, 1990.

MacKinnon, Catherine A. *Toward a Feminist Theory of the State.* Cambridge, Mass.: Harvard University Press, 1989.

Mahillon, Pierre. "Isabelle de Charrière." *La Nouvelle Revue Française* 326 (March 1980): 104–7.

Mat-Hasquin, Michèle. "Dramaturgie et démistification dans les comédies d'Isabelle de Charrière." *Etudes sur le XVIIIe siècle* 8 (1981): 53–66.

Mercier, Michel. *Le Roman féminin*. Paris: Presses universitaires de France, 1976.

Miller, Nancy K. "The Exquisite Cadavers: Women in Eighteenth-Century Fiction." Review of *La Destinée féminine*, by Pierre Fauchery. *Diacritics* 5 (1975): 37–43.

———. *The Heroine's Text: Readings in the French and English Novel, 1722–1782*. New York: Columbia University Press, 1980.

———. "Men's Reading, Women's Writing: Gender and the Rise of the Novel." *Yale French Studies* 75 (1988): 40–55.

———. "Men's Reading, Women's Writing: Gender and the Rise of the Novel." In *Displacements: Women, Tradition, Literatures in French*, edited by Joan DeJean and Nancy K. Miller, 37–54. Baltimore: The Johns Hopkins University Press, 1991.

———. "Rereading as a Woman: the Body in Practice." In *The Female Body in Western Culture: Contemporary Perspectives*, edited by Susan Rubin Suleiman, 354–61. Cambridge, Mass.: Harvard University Press, 1985.

———. *Subject to Change: Reading Feminist Writing*. New York: Columbia University Press, 1988.

———. "The Text's Heroine: a Feminist Critic and her Fictions." *Diacritics* 12 (1982): 48–53.

Minier-Birk, Sigyn. *Madame de Charrière: Les premiers romans*. Paris: Champion-Slatkine, 1987.

Moi, Toril. "Feminist, Female, Feminine." In *The Feminist Reader: Essays in Gender and the Politics of Literary Criticism*, edited by Catherine Belsey and Jane Moore. New York: Basil Blackwell, 1989.

Moser-Verrey, Monique. "Isabelle de Charrière en quête d'une meilleure entente." *Stanford French Review* 11 (1987): 63–76.

Mylne, Vivienne. *The Eighteenth-Century French Novel: Techniques of Illusion*. 2d ed. Cambridge: Cambridge University Press. 1981.

Oates, Joyce Carol. "Is There a Female Voice? Joyce Carol Oates Replies." *Women and Literature* 1 (1980): 10–11.

O'Brien, Sharon. "Feminist Theory and Literary Biography." In *Contesting the Subject: Essays in the Postmodern Theory and Practice of Biography and Biographical Criticism,* edited by William H. Epstein, 123–33. West Lafayette, Ind.: Purdue University Press, 1991.

Offen, Karen. "The New Sexual Politics of French Revolutionary Historiography." *French Historical Studies* 16 (1990): 909–22.

Outram, Dorinda. *The Body and the French Revolution: Sex, Class, and Political Culture.* New Haven: Yale University Press, 1989.

Parker, Alice. "Madame de Tencin and the 'Mascarade' of Female Im/personation." *Eighteenth-Century Life* 9 (1985): 65–78.

Pateman, Carole. *The Sexual Contract.* Cambridge, U. K.: Polity Press, 1988.

Pelckmans, Paul. "La fausse emphase de la 'mort de toi.'" *Neophilogus* 72 (1988): 498–515.

Reid, Roddey. *Families in Jeopardy: Regulating the Social Body in France, 1750–1910.* Stanford, Calif.: Stanford University Press, 1993.

Rosbottom, Ronald C. "The Novel and Gender Difference." In *A New History of French Literature,* edited by Denis Hollier, 481–87. Cambridge, Mass.: Harvard University Press, 1989.

Rossard, Janine. "Le Désir de mort romantique dans *Caliste.*" *PMLA* 87, no. 3 (May 1972): 492–98.

Rousseau, Jean-Jacques. *Emile, or on Education.* Translated by Allan Bloom. New York: Basic Books, Inc., 1979.

Schor, Naomi. "*Triste Amérique*: *Atala* and the Postrevolutionary Construction of Woman." In *Rebel Daughters: Women and the French Revolution,* edited by Sara E. Melzer and Leslie W. Rabine, 139–56. New York: Oxford University Press, 1992.

Scott, Joan Wallach. "'A Woman Who Has only Paradoxes to Offer': Olympe de Gouges Claims Rights for Women." In *Rebel Daughters: Women and the French Revolution,* edited by Sara E. Melzer and Leslie W. Rabine, 102–20. New York: Oxford University Press, 1992.

Showalter, English, Jr. "Madame de Graffigny and her Salon." *Studies in Eighteenth-Century Culture* 6 (1977): 377–91.

Smith, Barbara Herrnstein. "Value/Evaluation." In *Critical Terms for Literary Study,* edited by Frank Lentricchia and Thomas McLaughlin, 177–85. Chicago: The University of Chicago Press, 1990.

Stanley, Liz. "Process in Feminist Biography and Feminist Epistemology." In *All Sides of the Subject; Women and Biography,* edited by Teresa Iles, 109–25. New York: Teachers College Press, 1992.

Starobinski, Jean. "Les *Lettres écrites de Lausanne* de Madame de Charrière: inhibition psychique et interdit social." In *Roman et lumières au XVIIIe siècle,* edited by Werner Krauss, 130–51. Paris: Editions Sociales, 1970.

Stewart, Joan Hinde. "Designing Women." In *A New History of French Literature,* edited by Denis Hollier, 553–58. Cambridge, Mass.: Harvard University Press, 1989.

———. *Gynographs: French Novels by Women of the Late Eighteenth Century.* Lincoln: University of Nebraska Press, 1993.

Stewart, Philip. *Imitation and Illusion in the French Memoir-Novel, 1700–1750.* New Haven: Yale University Press, 1969.

Trousson, Raymond. "Isabelle de Charrière et Jean-Jacques Rousseau." *Bulletin de l'Académie Royale de Langue et de Littératures Françaises* 43, No. 1 (1985): 5–57.

———. *Isabelle de Charrière, un destin de femme au XVIIIe siècle.* Paris: Hachette, 1994.

Vallois, Marie-Claire. "Exotic Femininity and the Rights of Man: *Paul et Virginie* and *Atala*, or the Revolution in Stasis." In *Rebel Daughters: Women and the French Revolution,* edited by Sara E. Melzer and Leslie W. Rabine, 178–97. New York: Oxford University Press, 1992.

Vercruyesse, Jerome. "Histoire et théâtre chez Isabelle de Charrière." *Revue d'histoire littéraire de la France* 85, no. 6 (1985): 978–87.

Vissière, Isabelle. "Duo épistolaire ou duel idéologique? La correspondance de Madame de Charrière et de Benjamin Constant pendant la Révolution." In *Benjamin Constant et la Révolution Française,* 39–60. Geneva: Droz, 1989.

West, Anthony. *Mortal Wounds.* London: Robson, 1975.

Whatley, Janet. "Isabelle de Charrière (1740–1805)." In *French Women Writers: A Bio-Bibliographical Source Book,* edited by Eva Martin Sartori and Dorothy Wynne Zimmerman, 35–46. Westport, Conn.: Greenwood Press, 1991.

Wilson, Lindsay. *Women and Medecine in the French Enlightenment; The Debate over 'Maladies des femmes'.* Baltimore: The Johns Hopkins University Press, 1993.

Index

DATE DUE

MAY 23 1996	

UPI 261-2505 G   PRINTED IN U.S.A.